CULTURES OF THE WORLD

Papua New Guinea

Cavendish Square

New York

Published in 2018 by Cavendish Square Publishing, LLC
243 5th Avenue, Suite 136, New York, NY 10016
Copyright © 2018 by Cavendish Square Publishing, LLC

Third Edition

Library of Congress Cataloging-in-Publication Data

Names: Gascoigne, Ingrid, author. | Schumacher, Cassandra, author.
Title: Papua New Guinea / Ingrid Gascoigne and Cassandra Schumacher.
Description: New York : Cavendish Square, 2018. | Series: Cultures of the world (third edition) | Audience: Grades 5-8. | Includes bibliographical references and index.
Identifiers: LCCN 2017046637 (print) | LCCN 2017047978 (ebook) | ISBN 9781502636300 (library bound) | ISBN 9781502636317 (ebook)
Subjects: LCSH: Papua New Guinea--Juvenile literature.
Classification: LCC DU740 (ebook) | LCC DU740 .G362 2018 (print) | DDC 995.3--dc23
LC record available at https://lccn.loc.gov/2017046637

Editorial Director: David McNamara
Editor: Kristen Susienka
Copy Editor: Nathan Heidelberger
Associate Art Director: Amy Greenan
Designer: Alan Sliwinski
Production Coordinator: Karol Szymczuk
Photo Research: J8 Media

PICTURE CREDITS

Printed in the United States of America

CONTENTS

PAPUA NEW GUINEA TODAY

PAPUA NEW GUINEA IS A NATION TRANSCENDING TIME. Consisting of a series of islands in the South Pacific, it went for millennia without outside influence, largely untouched by the outside world until the late sixteenth century. This area was a late prospect in the quest for colonization of the seventeenth and eighteenth centuries, and somehow stood outside the influence of westernization. The nearly impenetrable forest and terrain of the islands allowed many of Papua New Guinea's people to remain insulated and essentially cut off from outside forces for many years. Today, however, as almost every reach of this planet is, Papua New Guinea is a modern land still richly driven by tradition. With a proud oral history, a gradually growing written history, and a complex village and tribal structure within a modern commonwealth state, Papua New Guinea has worked hard to establish itself as a parliamentary democracy since its independence in 1975. It is a nation all its own, still working to build itself within its postcolonial era—not an easy feat considering how diverse a nation Papua New Guinea is.

Consisting of more than eight hundred villages with more than eight hundred languages spoken, Papua New Guinea has a unique and diverse culture that spans six hundred islands and archipelagoes in the South Pacific. The population is ever growing and is currently about 8 million people, a huge increase in population from the count at 2.8 million at the time of independence. In the face of modernization, Papua New Guinea works to maintain its traditional tribal structure and culture in an ever-changing, modern world.

The landscape is varied and beautiful, with mountain ranges, plains, fertile valleys, rain forests, and swamplands. Issues like sustainability and modernization bring with them unique challenges to the wildlife and people of the nation. Bright birds of paradise and insects abound, along with small mammals and crocodiles. It is a tropical oasis. The temperatures span from high and humid in the lowlands to cooler in the mountains, but are unified by the wet and dry seasons that impact an economy predominantly driven by subsistence farming.

The people of Papua New Guinea are diverse and have a rich tradition of gift giving that has progressed into feelings of community responsibility. To give is a way of life here. There is a strong tradition of sharing wealth, which allows for the community as a whole to thrive. For every village there is a unique way of interacting with the world. The rough terrain keeps people apart and has led to unique, independent communities that collectively are astounding, but it comes at a price. It is hard to unify a nation that is so intrinsically divided.

Art is also a way of life for these people. Song and dance tell the oral history of each tribe and act as regular entertainment. Such acts are just as suited in daily life as they are in festival celebrations. Song and dance also speak to the religious and supernatural traditions of the Papua New Guineans. Magic and spirits are believed to impact the daily lives of the people. Some traditional art is created in celebration of spirits and for ceremonial purposes. Traditional art forms like carvings and handmade masks are still valued for their presence at ceremonial dances and parties, as well as for artistic purposes and commercial sale.

Traditional farming methods are also having far-reaching impacts. Deforestation has endangered the varied wildlife, and problems with sustainability have arisen. There are vast resources in Papua New Guinea's islands, but they are very challenging to use and excavate. The trade of these resources makes up a vast portion of the economy, but it's a fine balance to use the land but not abuse the land.

Finding such a balance has Papua New Guinea coming out of an economic boom. The nation had been experiencing a period of economic growth and is now encountering an era of industrial expansion. However, there are problems facing

Papua New Guinea's capital, Port Moresby, is home to the Koki Market, which is filled with lush, local produce grown through subsistence farming.

it that will need to be resolved in the coming years. Education rates are low, and many adults in Papua New Guinea have insufficient formal schooling. Rising populations often lead to increased crime, and Papua New Guinea is not exempt. Urban areas and cities can be very dangerous. Low rates of employment and general poverty raise problems with petty crime. Traditional values and modern conveniences make for challenges for many members of the population.

Today, the country's political climate is experiencing tension. Recent elections of high-level officials are tainted with allegations of corruption, and significant civil unrest has resulted. Papua New Guinea has had independence since the 1970s, but it is still working today to define what that independence looks like. The vast array of islands ensures diversity within the culture and presents challenges in creating a unified nation.

Papua New Guinea is a land in tropical paradise. It is home to modern tourism as well as tall mountainous land still farmed as it was hundreds of years ago. Modern technologies like smartphones and the internet are changing the ways people live, but tradition stands strong. Tribal life is passionately maintained in some areas, but it is fighting a battle against the conveniences of modernity. Papua New Guinea is an ever-changing nation built on the foundation of steadfast people dedicated to their history.

GEOGRAPHY

This aerial view of the city of Lae in Morobe Province shows some of the diversity of the Papua New Guinea landscape. Lae is a coastal town, but tall mountains can be seen in the distance.

1

P APUA NEW GUINEA IS SIMPLY stunning. The Pacific region is riddled with beautiful vistas of mountains coated in thick jungle and tropical beaches. With birds of paradise dotting the canopy, it is easy to believe that this nation is paradise, but the thick jungles make navigating the terrain and using the bountiful resources challenging. The natural barriers ensure that each village and tribe is unique and different because their contact with each other was limited for thousands of years. There is great diversity in the land and the people because of the incredible geography of this nation.

THE LAND

In Papua New Guinea, there are more than six hundred small islands and archipelagoes, along with the "mainland," the eastern section of the large island known as New Guinea. Situated just south of the equator, it lies to the north of Australia, at the edge of the Pacific Ocean. The Torres Strait—the narrowest point between mainland Australia and

"Papua New Guinea has a remarkable range of natural environments, ranging from alpine ranges and mountain tops rising to 4,400 meters (14,436 feet) above sea-level, through montane forests on volcanic or karst pavements, to hot and humid lowland rainforests, savannahs and swamps that may extend for hundreds of kilometers along the wide coastal plains."
—Secretariat of the Pacific Regional Environment Programme

The highlands of Papua New Guinea are some of the most remote parts of the country because of the difficulties traversing the thick jungle.

Papua New Guinea—is about 100 miles (161 kilometers) across. One of the Australian-owned Torres Strait Islands lies less than 12.4 miles (20 km) from mainland Papua New Guinea.

To the east of Papua New Guinea lie the Solomon Islands, and to the north lie the Federated States of Micronesia. To the west, Papua New Guinea shares the island of New Guinea with the Indonesian provinces of Papua and West Papua. The Australian and Indonesian governments in 1968 agreed upon the border separating the two countries without consulting the indigenous communities. This border has been carefully mapped, but it passes through such rugged areas that little of its 512-mile (824 km) length is patrolled effectively by either country. The ties between the indigenous communities on both sides of the border are still strong, ensuring regular passage over the border for customary visits and to see relatives. That said, the Free Papua Movement, a group of anti-Indonesian guerrillas who protest Indonesian rule over the western half of the island, also sometimes cross the border to avoid Indonesian authorities. The tight bond between people on both sides enables this because travelers use traditional border cards to cross rather than passports. Increasing border security was an ongoing discussion as of 2017.

The total land area of Papua New Guinea is 174,850 square miles (452,860 square kilometers)—slightly larger than California. Of that landmass, about 85 percent is mainland. The remaining 15 percent consists of islands, the larger of which are New Britain and the independent region of Bougainville. Some of these islands are the submerged eastern end of a curved mountain chain that begins in the Himalayas and continues through Malaysia and into the Pacific. Some islands are within the Pacific Ring of Fire, an area of earthquakes and volcanic activity that forms a large circle in the

Pacific Ocean. Others are coral atolls—islands formed by the accumulation of the exoskeletons of many generations of coral. These atolls are usually ring- or horseshoe-shaped and surround a shallow lagoon.

THE HIGHLANDS

The mainland is bisected from east to west by a spine of jagged and steep mountains reaching heights of more than 13,000 feet (3,962 m). Temporary paths, such as the Kokoda Track, were cut through the mountains during World War II by fighting factions, but the ranges are not crossed by a permanent road. The only way to travel between north and south is by airplane or on foot. Despite the isolation, the central highland valleys are among the most fertile and heavily populated areas of the country. The tribal people living there were not discovered by European explorers until as late as the 1930s, and they still maintain a largely traditional way of life.

In some areas, the mountains graduate into rolling foothills extending to the sea, but elsewhere the coastline is largely fringed with mangroves. To the west are large, flat, and sparsely wooded grasslands with abundant rainfall and wildlife.

FAST RIVERS AND WETLANDS

The mainland is laced with a network of rivers that flow from the central mountains to the coast. The largest are the nearly 700-mile (1,127 km)

"On the mainland alone, there may be as many as 20,000 species of flowering plant."
—Neil Nightingale, in his book *New Guinea, an Island Apart*

THE ROADS OF PAPUA NEW GUINEA

Despite the mountainous terrain, roads link many towns. The construction of such roads is a difficult and expensive operation. The longest road is the Highlands (or Okuk) Highway, running 380 miles (612 km) from Lae to Mount Hagen in the central highlands and then onto Tari and Porgera. New roads have not been built since 2000, with a majority of efforts consisting of maintaining and rebuilding the current roads that are often damaged by natural disasters like landslides and floods.

PAPUA NEW GUINEA

SOUTH PACIFIC OCEAN

Admiralty Is
Manus Lorengau
St Matthias Group
New Hanover
Bismarck
Archipelago
Vanimo
Aitape
Wewak
Ambunti
Anjoram
Kavieng
New Ireland
Namatanai
Bismarck Sea
Karkar I.
Madang
Long I.
Umboi I.
Rabaul
Kokopo
New Britain
Kimbe
Kandrian
Buka I.
Buka
Bougainville
Arawa
Panguna
Buin
INDONESIA
Wabag
Mount Hagen
Tari Ialibu Kundiawa
Mendi
Goroka
Kainantu
Lae
Finschhafen
Kiunga
L. Murray
Huon
Gulf
Bulolo
Wau
Solomon Sea
SOLOMON ISLANDS
Balimo
Kerema
Morehead
Daru
Gulf of Papua
Kokoda
Popondetta
Trobriand Is
Woodlark I.
PORT MORESBY
D'Entrecasteaux Islands
Goodenough I.
Fergusson I.
Torres Strait
Alotau
Normanby I.
Louisiade Archipelago
Misima I.
AUSTRALIA
Coral Sea
Tagula I.
Rossel I.

This map of Papua New Guinea shows the country's island nature.

Sepik River, which heads toward the Bismarck Sea in the north, and the Fly River, which flows southward into the Gulf of Papua. These rivers are usually fast flowing, navigable, and provide a useful alternative to the rough land routes.

The Sepik is bordered by large expanses of swamp. Nonetheless, the Sepik region, which includes the river, its tributaries, and the surrounding villages, is well populated and noted as a center for traditional art. The uppermost reaches of the Sepik, among the most isolated parts of the country, have witnessed little change and remain relatively untouched by Western influence.

PAPUA NEW GUINEA'S ISLAND ORIGINS

The island of New Guinea is thought to have been part of the supercontinent of Gondwanaland, which included Australia, Antarctica, Africa, and South America. The supercontinent started breaking up sixty-five million years ago, and many of the plant and animal species found throughout Asia, Australia, the Pacific, and even Africa can be found in Papua New Guinea. The mountains contrast with the low-lying areas because of the differences in temperature and rainfall, and different plant types have adapted to the conditions at each altitude.

The peaks of the highest mountains are occasionally white with snow, but this is the exception. Above 11,000 feet (3,353 m), the mountains are covered with a type of alpine woodland that is similar to the tundra in North America. There are tussock grasses, low shrubs, tree ferns, southern pine, and native cedar. Many of the tiny flowers have close relatives as far away

IN THE "RING OF FIRE"

Papua New Guinea lies within the volcanic and earthquake-prone belt that circles the Pacific, running through Japan, Indonesia, New Zealand, and New Guinea. There are 450 active or dormant volcanoes within the "Ring of Fire." Papua New Guinea has 67 of them. These volatile, erupting natural wonders are an ever-present threat to the people who live near them. Though activity is not exactly regular, according to Wired *writer Erik Klemetti, "The volcanoes of the island nation have produced some of the largest eruptions in the past few millennia."*

Lava flows very slowly, and although evacuations allow people to outrun it, the lava can do much damage to forests, roads, and buildings. Well-planned emergency procedures can save entire populations, but not always homes. Falling ash can bury entire towns, but this normally happens over an extended period, and ash fall needs to be very thick before it becomes difficult for people to breathe. Despite the destruction they cause, volcanoes provide rich soil minerals. To farmers living in the area, this is a silver lining to an ash-filled cloud.

as the Himalayas and the Alps. Lichens and mosses tint the landscape with spectacular hues of white, purple, gray, red, and pink. Some areas can be boggy, and rich organic soils, such as peat, are widespread.

Farther down the slopes, at an altitude of between 11,000 and 6,600 feet (3,353 and 2,012 m), are the montane forests. These forests are similar to the highlands of New Zealand or Scotland, something unexpected on a tropical island. Here conifers and southern beech trees predominate, with an underlayer of large ferns and fungi. Furthermore, trees can support up to four hundred species of epiphytes (plants that live on a host plant but do not feed off it), such as orchids, mosses, and ferns.

Vegetation is thick throughout most of Papua New Guinea, but at the higher altitudes the trees grow stunted and twisted, keeping with the dark and gloomy atmosphere. Oak trees and pandani (also called screw pines)

are common, giving way to the lower montane forests at above 3,300 feet (1,006 m), where timber trees like hoop and klinki pines are dominant species.

The valleys and lowlands that cover more than 65 percent of Papua New Guinea are primarily tropical rain forest. The travel site Papua New Guinea: A Million Different Journeys describes Papua New Guinea as a "stunning tropical wonderland ... home to the largest area of intact rainforest outside of the Amazon." Massive trees form a canopy, and many palm trees, bamboos, pandani, and canes compete for sunlight. The plants grow rapidly with the high temperatures and ample water supply, and some trees reach 150 feet (46 m) in height. Vines and climbers such as rattan and strangler figs add to the tangle of greenery. These are among the most fertile places in Papua New Guinea. The villagers clear small patches of ground to grow sweet potatoes and bananas.

The lowland regions, particularly around the rivers, have large areas of swampy woodlands. In some areas, the grass appears to float on the constantly sodden earth. The residents harvest sago (a starchy palm used for food), wild sugarcane, and *pitpit* (a sturdy cane used in the building of homes). At the western end of mainland Papua New Guinea and in the drier areas around Port Moresby, the landscape becomes a savanna woodland similar to that of northern Australia. Dry grasses and thinly placed trees like eucalyptus grow here.

SPEAKING IN PAPUA NEW GUINEA

An excellent example of the diversity of the nation can be found within the spoken word. Papua New Guinea's linguistic heritage is diverse and varied, with more than eight hundred languages. Twelve percent of the world's languages are spoken here. Considering the size of the nation in relation to the rest of the world, that is incredible. The small size of the nation combined with the diversity of the languages ensures that only a few people share a language. According to World Population Review, *"Most languages have fewer than 1,000 speakers."*

THE CAPITAL

Papua New Guinea's capital, Port Moresby, had a population of about 345,000 people in 2015, making it the country's largest town. Sited on a natural harbor, it was formerly the administrative headquarters of British New Guinea and remained so when the territory was amalgamated with Australian New Guinea after World War II. When the country gained its independence in 1975, Port Moresby's status as the capital became more culturally meaningful. The central government offices, Parliament House, the University of Papua

Port Moresby, which is depicted here with children playing in the street, as well as other urbans centers, can be busy, with close quarters and access to Western amenities.

New Guinea, the National Museum and Art Gallery, and an international airport are located there.

The national buildings are large, modern buildings spread out on spacious grounds, but Port Moresby has shantytowns too. People are lured to the city by the seemingly prosperous lifestyle, but many end up living in squalid conditions among the squatters. Violence and crime are high, and gangs of young, male bandits called "rascals," who operate all over the country, are particularly active in impoverished urban areas with high unemployment. Port Moresby has been named the worst place to live multiple times because of the bad health care and gang violence. It is a city with high rates of unemployment and has one of the highest rates of crime in the world. The Economist Intelligence Unit placed Port Moresby sixth on their 2016 list of the world's least livable cities.

URBAN CENTERS AND CITIES

Papua New Guinea has a few larger cities and urban areas. These are some of the main ones.

LAE This prosperous shipping center has a deeper natural harbor and more central location than Port Moresby. The original town was destroyed in the effort to expel a Japanese presence here during World War II, but Lae was rebuilt farther inland. It has road links with the fertile highlands, where cash crops like coffee and tea are grown, and has often been suggested as an alternative site for the nation's capital. It has a high unemployment rate among its population, however, and petty crime is prevalent. One hill, Mount

Lunaman, a Japanese lookout during World War II, is riddled with tunnels and caves that are now occupied by dangerous "rascals."

MADANG With a population of over 29,000, it has often been called the prettiest town in the Pacific. It is geared toward the tourist trade. Unfortunately, the northern coastal port lost much of its business to Lae when the Highlands Highway, running from Lae to the central highlands, opened. It has, however, captured the area's logging trade to support its economy.

The smaller town of Madang is known for its beautiful vistas and coastal waters.

WEWAK AND GOROKA These two towns (18,230 and 18,503 inhabitants, respectively) were useful to the Europeans as trading points, pawns, and strategic locations during World War II. They thrive because of trade, attracting a large mix of cultural groups.

The town of Wewak, located on the Sepik River, is a trade locale for the country.

THE FAUNA

New Guinea and Australia are thought to have been joined as recently as six thousand years ago. Because of this, they share many animal species, particularly marsupials—mammals whose young develop inside pouches found on their mother's stomach. Wallabies, tree kangaroos, bandicoots, possums, and echidnas are found in both countries.

Double-wattled cassowaries, ostrich-like birds, live in New Guinea, most often in the rain forest, though occasionally they stray to swampy, forested areas. Some tribes hunt them for their meat, which is considered a delicacy. Their feathers are used to decorate headdresses, and the feather quills are used for earrings. These animals have been traded throughout Asia for at least five hundred years. For some native clans, cassowaries are the subject of legends and are believed to have mystical powers.

A variety of wild dog similar to the Australian dingo, called the singing dog, is found in New Guinea. It is seldom seen but is heard howling at night in the highest parts of Papua New Guinea. For many years, these wild dogs, considered to be of ancient origin, were thought to be extinct in the wild, but in 2017 a group of at least fifteen wild singing dogs was located and photographed.

Additionally, domesticated dogs are kept as pets and to aid in hunting. Pigs are also domesticated and were brought to Papua New Guinea about six thousand years ago, most likely by immigrants or traders from Southeast Asia. They play an important part in the life of a village. While some Papua New Guineans, especially the Seventh-Day Adventists, do not eat pigs, other Papua New Guineans feast on them. Many consider pigs as an indispensable part of the family and see them as symbols of wealth. Pigs are spoken to and are given names. Women harvesting sweet potatoes often lead pigs to the fields, where they are let loose to root for remaining tubers. Not only are the pigs fed this way, but they also help to till the soil, which must otherwise be done manually.

The cassowary is a large, tropical bird similar to an ostrich that is hunted for meat and whose feathers are valued for ritual purposes.

FAUNA IN FLIGHT

Papua New Guinea has one of the richest and most diverse bird populations in the world, and many of the birds have been declared national animals. There are more species of kingfishers, pigeons, and parrots here than anywhere else. Other birds include hornbills, big palm cockatoos, and cassowaries. The birds feast on the fruits, nuts, nectar, and pollen that in other countries are eaten by monkeys and other primates or squirrels. The most famous bird, which appears on the country's flag and coat of arms, is the beautifully plumed bird of paradise. Of the forty-three species of this bird, thirty-eight are found in Papua New Guinea. Its feathers can be seen decorating the elaborate headdresses of the indigenous people.

Perhaps most spectacular of all of Papua New Guinea's fauna is its variety of insects. With a wingspan of up to 10.6 inches (27 centimeters), the Hercules moth is the world's largest moth and is found here. There are also giant millipedes, sticklike insects that reach more than 12 inches (30 cm) in length, and breathtaking birdwing butterflies. Of the eleven birdwing species documented, eight are found in Papua New Guinea. The female Queen Alexandra's birdwing has a wingspan of up to 12 inches (30 cm). Another insect that invites curiosity is the fiercely territorial antlered fly, found only in northern Australia and Papua New Guinea. The males have a large antler-like structure protruding from their heads, which they use as a defensive display. Some insects, such as green scarab beetles, are used by the natives as body ornaments.

Conservation efforts have varied through the years. In the early 2000s, scientists bred insects for conservation. Since then, many unusual insects continue to be collected for research purposes in the face of deforestation.

The palm cockatoo, shown here, is just one of many diverse and brightly colored birds found in the tree canopies of Papua New Guinea.

AVIAN CONSERVATION

Early European and Asian traders were quick to exploit the unusual wildlife, paying local people to hunt for the spectacular and rare hides and feathers, which were exported and sold for a high price. This decimated many species on the islands. Much of Papua New Guinea's wildlife is now recognized as a valuable asset because of this, and since the 1920s, many species have been declared national animals and protected by legislation. Such animals can only be hunted by traditional methods for tribal use. Commercial and sport hunting of these animals is illegal, and the penalties for transgressors are stiff. Furthermore, the daily life of the tribal landowners is inextricably tied to their surroundings. There are traditions and laws that conserve the natural resources on which they depend for their livelihood.

The Wilson's bird of paradise is one of almost forty species of birds of paradise to be found in Papua New Guinea.

FROM THE SEA

The coastal areas are lined with swampy marshes teeming with plants adapted to living in the salty tidal conditions. They act as a haven for fish and prawns to breed, and trees can grow up to 100 feet (30 m) high. The seawater is often heavily silted because of runoff from the steep slopes that high rainfall sends into the rivers and sea.

Divers consider Papua New Guinea one of the best dive sites in the world. The area also provides an ideal habitat for sea grass, a land plant that has adapted to living in salt water. It grows where the water is too deep for mangroves but too murky for coral, and supports a huge number of sea creatures, including the herbivorous dugong, or sea cow. The dugongs are large, slow, docile marine mammals that can be up to 9 feet (2.7 m) in length. They inhabit shallow coastal waters but can no longer be found in many of their former haunts. They are considered a threatened species, with fewer than one hundred thousand of them left in the world.

There are also several varieties of marine turtle caught by the coastal people, including the green turtle for its meat and the hawksbill for its shell. Fly River has its own pig-nosed turtle, which can be seen on the country's five-toea coin. Whales, dolphins, corals, venomous sea snakes, and an abundance of yet unclassified marine creatures fascinate divers and marine biologists alike.

A dugong forages the ocean floor for bits of vegetation to eat.

THE CLIMATE

Temperatures are high in most of Papua New Guinea's lowland areas and along the coast, with maximum temperatures averaging 90 degrees Fahrenheit (32 degrees Celsius). The highland areas are much cooler at 72—77°F (22—25°C).

For the most part, the country experiences two main seasons, the wet and the dry. However, there is so much rain in some areas that the land is never dry at all but merely less sodden. The northwest monsoon brings rain from December to March, and southeasterly trade winds blow from May to

NEW DISCOVERIES

Papua New Guinea's island nature and tropical climate lead to incredible diversity in its animals and plants. According to the World Wildlife Fund, "Here [in New Guinea], in just 1% of the world's land area, live at least 5% of the world's species. Two-thirds of these are unique to New Guinea." In 2015, the islands of Manus and Mussau, the northernmost islands of Papua New Guinea, were explored by a team of scientists from the Wildlife Conservation Society. There the scientists discovered many new and unfamiliar species like the leaf-nosed bat from the islands' limestone cliffs. There was also a new lizard, the forest dragon, discovered with very long toes and tails.

Plants like the bedstraw plant and the pandanus palm, with its bright-red fruit, were also found. This is just a small fraction of the animals and plants to be explored in Papua New Guinea, some of which have yet to be discovered.

THE RAIN FORESTS

The island of New Guinea has one of the largest spans of intact rain forests in the world; only the Amazon rain forest is larger. Sixty-five percent of the island is covered in forest. There are lowland and montane rain forests. In the highlands, the Central Range montane forests rise up over the mountainous terrain.

This forest is divided into three different vegetation zones, including the lower montane forest, the upper montane forest, and the high montane forest. Each zone contains different flora and fauna. Trees like oaks and laurels can be found in the lower montane, while Nothofagus *(southern beeches) are common in the upper montane. The high montane is more sparse because of the high altitude and is home to more conifers. Unique animals like the Cyclops long-beaked echidna and the Scott's tree kangaroo reside in the montane forests, along with the northern glider. The lowland rain forests are more habitable to animals than the montane forests, which are not as populated because of the high altitudes.*

The lowland forests, such as the Southern New Guinea lowland rain forests and the Vogelkop-Aru lowland rain forests, also have an incredible plant life, with 1,200 species of trees and 2,000 different ferns. The spangled kookaburra and the endemic lowland tree kangaroo make their homes there among the resident 69 mammalian species and 344 bird species.

One of the greatest challenges facing Papua New Guinea can also be found in the rain forests. Logging of the rain forest is a conservation issue in the twenty-first century. Research completed by Russian physicists states, "Papua New Guinea's forests contribute to the maintenance of the current favourable [sic] climate regime … Their devastation could trigger adverse changes in local, regional, and possibly global climates." Preservation of the forests helps ensure global well-being. Tourists also appreciate the incredible landscapes, and the government is capitalizing on the ectotourism trade within their forests. The rich biodiversity is singular and unique, allowing visitors to appreciate a plethora of different flora and fauna. Extensive hiking trails, including the 60-mile (97 km) Kokoda Trail, draw hikers and adventurers to the nation so that they may experience the rich beauty of the island.

October, bringing drier and cooler weather. April and November are the most uncomfortable times because they are transition months. The mountains tend to capture much of the precipitation, sheltering some areas from the monsoons. The Port Moresby area has a definite dry season, with an annual average rainfall of 39 inches (1 m) that occurs in short bursts during the wet season. In Lae, the average rainfall is greater than 177 inches (4.5 m), falling mostly between May and October, with the wettest months being June, July, and August. In some areas (the western part of New Britain, parts of the Gulf of Papua, and some of the western provinces) there is year-round rain, and rainfall can average greater than 236 inches (6 m) per year. Papua New Guinea is wet, hot, and humid.

INTERNET LINKS

http://www.greenpeace.org/international/Global/international/code/2013/png/index.html
This Greenpeace link has a video that describes ecoforestry and how it is used in Papua New Guinea.

http://timlaman.com/photo-galleries/birds-of-paradise
This website shows various pictures of the beautiful and diverse birds of paradise of Papua New Guinea.

http://wwf.panda.org/what_we_do/where_we_work/new_guinea_forests/area_forests_new_guinea/plants_animals_new_guinea_forests
The World Wildlife Fund has a webpage that shows images and gives descriptions of many different species native to Papua New Guinea.

http://www.zoo.org/tkcp/wildlife
This website describes different animal species from Papua New Guinea, with additional pictures of the fauna.

HISTORY

This ceremonial *eharo* mask shows some of the rich, living cultural history of Papua New Guinea. Masks like these are traditionally created just for fun to amuse spectators watching ceremonial dancing at intervillage meetings.

2

PAPUA NEW GUINEA IS A LAND OF oral history. Relatively recent exposure to global influences has led to a written history, but for the natives, stories hold the key to the past. People such as the Enga of Papua New Guinea have oral histories that span back eight to ten generations and record long histories that were fact checked by anthropologists and found to be true. Though the history was not traditionally recorded, the oral preservation of stories and happenings was far reaching and diverse, and tells the history of a very diverse nation.

"The many thousands of years of human occupation of New Guinea has led to a great deal of ethnic diversity." —WWF Global

FIRST SETTLEMENTS

It is believed that people arrived on the New Guinea mainland as emigrants from eastern Indonesian islands as early as fifty thousand years ago, in the glacial period. Later arrivals came from other areas in Indonesia, Asia, and the South Pacific. These people were likely nomadic hunters and gatherers. Although New Guinea probably was once connected to Australia, part of the immigrants' journey involved crossing deep seawaters in canoes.

Unlike in other parts of the world, the development of agriculture in what is now Papua New Guinea did not cause the growth of larger political and social units such as cities and states. Instead, the tribe and the clan remained the basic social units. Because the basic food crops could not be stored for long periods due to climatic conditions, it was not possible to stockpile food for wealth, nor could farmers take time out to fight protracted wars to conquer neighboring territories. Short and ferocious battles were fought over territory and property, but these were conducted mainly in the valleys, with villages built defensively on the hillsides.

It is highly probable that new agricultural methods were introduced by farmers arriving from Southeast Asia. As tools were developed and crops introduced, larger groups of people settled in fixed locations. Archaeological discoveries include drainage channels in the highlands at a site in Kuk Swamp that indicate intensive use of agriculture around seven thousand years ago. Trenched roads, defensive gates, and ditches used for fighting have also been found in the southern highlands, indicating early tribal war. Between seventeen thousand and ten thousand years ago, climatic warming led to a worldwide melting of ice sheets, resulting in a gradual rise in sea levels, which covered the original land links with Australia. The grasslands decreased in size, and the forested areas increased.

THE TRADITION OF TRADING

Evidence suggests that New Guinea highlanders may have been among the world's first agriculturalists, growing crops of yams, bananas, and coconuts. Early farmers developed sophisticated techniques to obtain maximum yields without metal tools, including composting dead vegetation to add nutrients to the soil and a system of crop rotation.

Long before Europeans arrived, Papua New Guinea used a trade-based economy, both locally and with other lands. Overland and inter-island trade routes existed for the exchange of sago, pottery, shells, salt, and stone axes. Large seagoing trade expeditions, called *hiri* (hih-REE), launched by the Motu in the Port Moresby area, traded pots for sago and canoe logs in the Gulf of Papua. Subsequent trade with Asia lasted one thousand years, in which Chinese merchants and sea captains were the middlemen in exchanges of Asian glass beads, metal goods, cloth, and porcelain for New Guinean tree bark, spices, and exotic bird feathers.

Steel axes, which preceded the arrival of European settlers, were traded inland. They were more efficient than stone axes for clearing gardens and making canoes. Use of the steel axes increased leisure time for the men, which eventually led to frequent tribal wars.

This drawing shows the British raising their flag, the Union Jack, in Papua New Guinea in 1885 during their annexation.

EUROPEAN INFLUENCE AND COLONIZATION

Although the people of the area knew of the Malay and Chinese through raiding and the taking of slaves for centuries, the islands were untouched by

DRAINING A SWAMP

About nine thousand years ago, large parts of the Wahgi swamp in the Western Highlands were drained to create farming land, an achievement remarkable for its time. The swamp was drained in six different stages and is used as evidence that Papua New Guinea has a long history of plant domestication.

This portrait shows
Jorge de Meneses.

European influence until the sixteenth century. Around 1526, the Portuguese sea captain Jorge de Meneses may have been the first European to land on the island. He named it Ilhas dos Papuas (Land of the Frizzy-Haired People). He was unimpressed with what he found—a difficult terrain with no apparent natural resources to encourage further exploration. Later, the Spaniard Iñigo Ortiz de Retes landed on the northeastern parts of the mainland in 1546 and named the land Nueva Guinea (New Guinea) because it reminded him of the Guinea Coast in Africa. Explorers largely ignored the island, as it lay away from direct sea routes at the time.

In 1793, Lieutenant John Hayes led the first European attempt at settlement. He claimed the entire island of New Guinea for Britain. He built a fortified settlement that he called Fort Coronation at the western end of New Guinea. It was used for trading in nutmeg trees, dyewood roots, and teak. The settlement was abandoned the following year after it flooded with monsoonal rains, was attacked by hostile locals, and fell victim to mosquito-borne diseases. The Dutch disputed the British claim and laid claim to the western half of New Guinea in 1828. As had happened to the British settlers, however, the Dutch were plagued with mosquitoes and the threat of malaria, and they deserted their outpost, Fort du Bus, in 1835. The Dutch continued to claim sovereignty over the western half of New Guinea until 1898 but were in reality too distant to monitor the territory.

Traders based in Australia showed the next interest in New Guinea. Whalers and sealers traded small axes, rum, beads, mirrors, and firearms for pearls, tortoiseshell, coconuts, hardwood, rubber, feathers, and copra. In areas that were used regularly by trading vessels, the local population became accustomed to the traders and learned to barter. This helped European traders set up bases in these areas. Other areas were taken by force. By the second quarter of the nineteenth century, most of New Guinea's coastline had been charted.

From the 1840s, parts of New Guinea, Milne Bay, and the Bismarck Archipelago became recruiting points for people supplying cheap labor to sugar plantations in Fiji, Samoa, and Australia. Conditions on the plantations were brutal, and the workers, called "blackbirds," were exploited. In the 1870s, Christian missionaries began to visit New Guinea and the surrounding islands. Their influence is reflected in the high percentage of Christians found in Papua New Guinea today.

In 1884, Germany claimed the northeastern area of New Guinea and the Bismarck Archipelago, setting up a trading post about 300 miles (483 km) up the Sepik River. Fearing a German move south toward their own coastline, the Australian colonies, which were otherwise independent of each other, got together and collectively pressured the British government to make its presence felt. That same year, Britain annexed the southeastern portion of New Guinea.

UNDER EUROPEAN RULE

The New Guinea Kompagnie initially administered the German colony. It was a trading company accorded the task of developing whatever land it could acquire on behalf of the German government. Germany passed the laws for the new territory, but its administration, development, and local matters were entrusted to the company. The company's main concern was profit. It established tobacco plantations in Astrolabe Bay and coconut plantations elsewhere.

The German government took over the company's rule in 1899, and the colony continued to be run for its plantations and trade value. The focus was on building roads and setting up administrative controls, but little was done for the local people who provided cheap labor for the German operations. A *luluai* (loo-loo-AY), or headman, in each village was authorized to collect taxes, settle minor disputes, report major disputes, and ensure that the villagers obeyed government orders. *Luluais* were assisted by *tultuls* (TUHL-tuhls), who acted as interpreters and go-betweens.

By 1908, the coconut plantations were maturing, copra exports boomed, and scientific expeditions had started to penetrate the inhospitable interior.

Very little of the Papua New Guinean mainland was explored by Europeans before World War I because of logistics problems. The mountains and jungles made travel inland incredibly challenging and limited vehicular transport. A porter could only carry up to 40 pounds (18 kilograms) of food, which was just enough for one person to live on for fourteen days, but this would not have been able to sustain prolonged European exploration of the area. The terrain was difficult, and navigating the rivers was not easy. The use of planes to airdrop food ended this restriction, and there was a boom in successful exploration from the 1920s onward.

The country's thick foliage and varied geology make travel into higher altitudes challenging.

Most of the territory was under the control of government stations and district officers. In 1914, Australian forces occupied the colony, and Germany lost control of it. In 1921, the League of Nations gave Australia mandate over the area, which was renamed the Territory of New Guinea.

When the British had annexed the southeastern area of New Guinea, including Port Moresby, in 1884, their immediate concern—like that of the Germans—had been to set up a governmental infrastructure within the colony. Their administrative structure was similar to that of the Germans, only instead of having *luluais*, the British established an armed constabulary into which Papuans were inducted as village constables. The area was divided into three divisions, each governed by a regional magistrate. The British protectorate was handed over to Australia in 1906, when it was renamed Papua. After World War I, Australia continued to govern both Papua and the Territory of New Guinea. Administrative control was based in Australia, where all the major decisions were made. These were then implemented by a mostly expatriate Australian staff located in Port Moresby and Rabaul.

WORLD WAR II IN THE PACIFIC

World War II arrived in the Papua and New Guinea territories in 1942. The invading Japanese planned to take Port Moresby and set it up as their southern outpost in Southeast Asia and the Pacific, to supply raw materials such as tin, rubber, and oil. The Japanese invasion in January 1942 was swift; the army quickly captured much of New Guinea's north coast and most of the surrounding islands. The Australian and American forces held on to Milne Bay and a few offshore islands, such as the Trobriands. However, the Japanese victory was short-lived. They came close to their original goal of Port Moresby but were driven back by Australian forces at Kokoda. By September 1942, the Japanese had started their long, slow retreat. The Allied forces finally recovered the mainland in 1945, and some islands were not reclaimed by Australian forces until after the atomic bombings of Hiroshima and Nagasaki.

The war fought in Papua New Guinea was a grim one. The soldiers traveled through the rugged and seemingly impassable terrain largely on foot and with minimal supplies. By 1942, the warring countries took to the air in an attempt to hasten their victories, starting a series of bombing raids that continued for three years. The devastating effects of war were felt by the local people—the

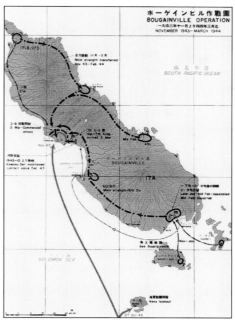

This map of Bougainville depicts the Japanese military movement over the island from November 1943 to March of 1944 during World War II.

STRIKING GOLD

In the 1920s, gold was found at Wau and Bulolo, and the exploration of the highlands began in earnest. The fledgling use of airplanes in the supply network meant that expeditions could venture farther into the inaccessible and more rugged territories than was previously possible. The Australians were astonished to find a civilization of nearly one million people in the highlands who remained untouched by the outside world. Despite the flurry of activity caused by gold mining, little infrastructural development took place during the decades preceding World War II.

European arrival in Papua New Guinea's highlands prior to World War II led to cargo cults. As early as the 1870s, these groups were taking shape. Planes and modern tools were alien in a land of stone-age technology. During European arrival and especially in World War II, foreigners brought "cargo"— resources, machines, and wealth. Among indigenous people witnessing these "miracles" for the first time, a belief arose that these foreign men had power over their goods

During World War II, military planes such as this C-47 carried supplies and goods into Papua New Guinea, which would lead to cargo cults.

because of religion, and wealth gave them power over the New Guinean people. Locals began wearing Western clothing and ritualizing the arrival of these cargo loads with religious fervor in hopes of gaining such power and wealth. Even though the wars ended and the foreigners left, their "cargo" in tow, cargo cults continued to persist and do so even today.

bombardment of their towns and villages destroyed canoes, trees, plants, and animals that they depended on for their livelihood. The danger of aerial attack and military restrictions on sea travel limited coastal fishing. The scarcity of food and other raw materials added to the hardship of living in a country at war.

STRIVING FOR AND GAINING INDEPENDENCE

In 1945, Australian colonel Jack Keith Murray was appointed the chief administrator of both territories, now called the Territory of Papua and New Guinea. His task was to establish health and education services, control local disputes, and liaise with plantation owners.

From 1946, Australia administered the territories under a United Nations mandate. Soon after, the push toward independence began. The First House of Assembly was formed in 1964 with sixty-four elected Papua New Guinean members. This group created the Select Committee on Constitutional Development to help prepare the region for independence. One of their recommendations included increasing the number of representatives to eighty-four in 1967. This also led to the Second House of Assembly in 1968, with ninety-four members. The Second House decided that the independent country would be known as Papua New Guinea. It set up a committee in 1972 to draft a constitution, and the Third House of Assembly was formed. On December 1, 1973, the territory obtained full self-government, and on September 16, 1975, the new constitution took effect. Australia's prime minister, Gough Whitlam, and Britain's Prince Charles attended the official change of flags before a crowd of ten thousand people in Port Moresby.

A NEW NATION

Not everyone in Papua New Guinea wanted independence. There was the problem of creating a sense of loyalty to the central government, located

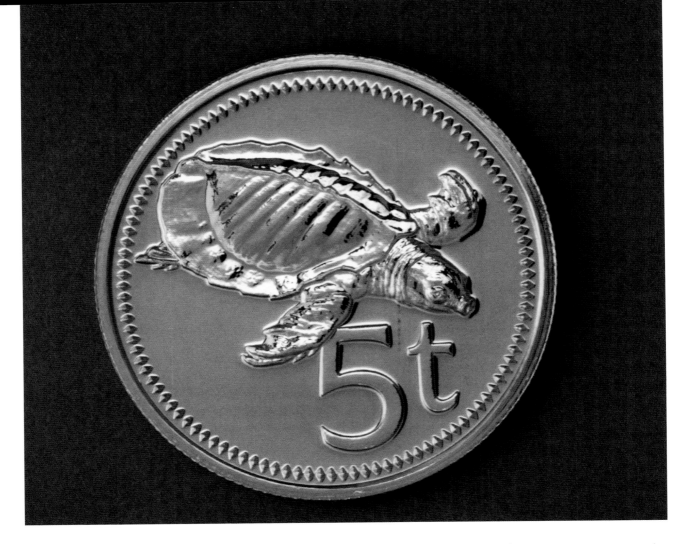

This five-toea coin, part of the country's currency, was first made in 1978, not long after Papua New Guinea gained independence.

in Port Moresby, far away from much of the population. To many people, the highlanders in particular, the government seemed removed from the day-to-day issues affecting them. In a sense, people in the remote villages were fearful of being dominated by others with a lifestyle that was more advanced. Some areas of the country were officially barred to travelers because of hostility from the indigenous people and cannibalistic practices. Since independence, the establishment of local governments and village courts has eased the tension.

However, the failure to create a sense of national identity resulted in numerous separatist movements that flared up periodically. An example from 1972 involved Josephine Abaijah, the first woman to be elected to the

The story of Papua New Guinea's flag is unique. In 1971, Papua New Guinea prepared for independence. One symbol that was of great importance was the country's flag. That year, there was a countrywide search for the design that would forever define the nation. The design would be based off of a crest that had been designed earlier.

At the age of fifteen, a student named Susan Karike, from Yule Island, encouraged by her art teacher, submitted her design. The Second House of Assembly would go on to vote on it and accept it as the official flag of Papua New Guinea. It was adopted on March 4, 1971.

The flag is black, red, and yellow. Karike chose those colors since they were the most commonly used in traditional ceremonies. The yellow bird of paradise soars above the Southern Cross, symbolizing the country's evolution into nationhood. The Southern Cross, a constellation found in the Southern Hemisphere, signifies Papua New Guinea's historical links with Australia and its goodwill toward its South Pacific neighbors.

House of Assembly. She pushed for the southern region of Papua to secede. She was supported by wealthy businesspeople of the region, who did not want to share their region's affluence with the whole country.

BOUGAINVILLE SECESSION AND DISSENT

Proponents of a secessionist movement on Bougainville Island argued that the island had stronger cultural and geographic ties with the Solomon Islands than with New Guinea. Bougainville's geographical location is very close to the Solomon Islands, which ensured stronger linguistic and cultural ties. The

Bougainville, as depicted here, and its independence is one of the most strongly contested issues in Papua New Guinea.

separation of Bougainville from the Solomon Islands was largely due to a poorly drawn map in the 1800s.

In 1964, Panguna—one of the locales on the island—was the site of a major copper discovery. More than $288 million was invested in the development of the mine and the surrounding infrastructure, including roads, a new town, a power station, and a seaport. By the time Papua New Guinea gained its independence, the mine was earning half of the country's internal revenue. Cultural distance, combined with tension over the Panguna mine revolving around modernization, income, environmental damages from mining, and feelings of governmental neglect to the region, led to a hotbed of discontent and calls for independence.

BOUGAINVILLE'S INDEPENDENCE

Meetings between Bougainville factions were held on neutral territory in New Zealand. A cooperative agreement was signed in 1998, recommending a cease-fire, total demilitarization of the area, and the establishment of an international peacekeeping force. The process culminated in the Bougainville Peace Agreement in 2001, with Bougainville being given immediate but limited self-government. Some twenty thousand people died before peace was achieved. The first elections for the autonomous Bougainville government were held in 2005, and on June 15, 2005, the new thirty-nine-member parliament was sworn in, with Joseph Kabui as the first president. In May 2017, Bougainville's president, John Momis, and Papua New Guinea's prime minister, Peter O'Neill, agreed to a referendum for Bougainville's independence on June 15, 2019. There is talk of reopening the Panguna copper mine in hopes of using revenue from the venture to fund independence.

Father John Momis headed the secessionist movement that escalated in 1976, and negotiations were held. The secessionists were assured they would exert a strong influence on the rest of the country and were allowed to set up the first provincial government. Thus persuaded, they reluctantly chose to remain within the jurisdiction of the national parliament, and things went well for a short time.

A small group of traditional landowners enjoyed huge royalties from mining, but little community development resulted. There was growing suspicion among the people that they had been short-changed in their earliest negotiations with Bougainville Copper Limited's parent company, CRA. In 1987, the Panguna Landowners Association was formed, led by Perpetua Serero and Francis Ona. It demanded stricter environmental measures, back payments in profits, and $10 billion in compensation. When CRA failed to meet these demands, the Bougainville Revolutionary Army began to sabotage the mine, which was closed in May 1989. This was a blow to Papua New Guinea's economy, though it was partially offset by the Ok Tedi copper and gold mine and other highland mines. A state of emergency was declared, and the situation deteriorated into a civil war that would last a decade.

In 2013, Papua New Guinea worked with Australia to create a refugee detainment camp on Manus Island. It was open for roughly four years, but with great tension. Detainees would eventually stage a hunger strike in protest of their treatment in the camp, and ultimately, when violence broke out later on, Papua New Guinea was forced to assess the camp through a human rights lens and found trouble. Papua New Guinea's Supreme Court ruled the detainment center unconstitutional. The government was forced to evacuate the refugees, but they adamantly refused to leave until a safe location for them to live was found. As of summer 2017, refugees remained on Manus Island, waiting for a safe place for relocation.

Early in 1997, the prime minister, Sir Julius Chan, and a few cabinet ministers hired a London-based mercenary group, Sandline Limited, for $36 million, to fight the Bougainville insurgents. Neither parliament nor the people were consulted. In March, Brigadier General Jerry Singirok, who spoke against the move, was fired for insubordination. The issue aroused national outrage and violence in the capital. Riot police were sent in, the Sandline contract was suspended, and the prime minister and his deputy resigned.

Bougainville today has an autonomous government, with a thirty-nine-member parliament led by a president. This province has its own judicial system, including supreme and high courts. A final vote for secession will take place in 2019.

RECENT ELECTONS

The most recent government elections have been plagued with trouble. In 2011, Prime Minister Michael Somare was suspended for two weeks on allegations of corruption. He eventually retired from his position. When he later returned to resume his position, stating that he was never actually willing to give up his seat, Peter O'Neill had already been put in office. A group of rebel soldiers seized the Port Moresby military headquarters in a demand that Somare be reinstated, but to no avail. The efforts to reinstate Somare ended with a vote because neither man would relinquish the position. O'Neill was the ultimate victor at the polls, and Somare was forced to drop his bid and support O'Neill. From there, O'Neill led the country for the following five years. During this time, O'Neill was accused of corruption as well, specifically relating to the misuse and misallocation of government funds. There was actually a warrant issued for his arrest, but rather than comply with the order, O'Neill disbanded the investigating anticorruption force, Taskforce Sweep, and replaced it.

This move and accusations of corruption followed O'Neill into the 2017 elections. O'Neill did manage to maintain his seat as the prime minister of Papua New Guinea, but his position came at a cost. Political dissatisfaction and rioting erupted before, during, and after the election, showing the instability and general dissatisfaction of many people in the nation.

INTERNET LINKS

http://www.abc.net.au/news/2015-09-16/timeline-of-papua-new-guinea-road-to-independence/6748374
At this website, explore the path to independence completed by Papua New Guinea.

http://www.bbc.com/news/world-asia-15593238
Read this interactive timeline of Papua New Guinea's history.

https://www.youtube.com/watch?v=lYIAt-1fDU8
This documentary explores the Australian and American presence in Papua New Guinea during World War II.

GOVERNMENT

Papua New Guinea's parliamentary building in Port Moresby has the long lines and design of the famous spirit houses in the Maprik region.

3

PAPUA NEW GUINEA HAS FACED some battles in government since its independence, but fundamentally, the nation is an independent state and a member of the British Commonwealth (also called the Commonwealth of Nations). The British monarch is its formal head of state. A governor-general stands for the reigning British monarch, but it is mostly a ceremonial position held by a citizen of Papua New Guinea.

As an independent state, Papua New Guinea makes its own laws and votes for its own government, including the members of parliament. The popular vote determines who wins seats in parliament. These representatives in turn elect the prime minister, generally the leader of the majority part of the single-chamber National Parliament. The executive power, according to the constitution, is held by the prime minister. However, parliament can limit the power of the executive branch with a no-confidence vote. According to a 2017 analysis by CountryWatch, "Intra-parliamentary disputes, arising from unstable political alliances and leading to frequent changes in government, are a typical and seemingly intractable feature on Papua New Guinea's political landscape." The nation's government changes regularly, which makes stability challenging.

"Elections in PNG (Papua New Guinea) are never a clean process, and in many ways are a tremendous celebration of the democratic process. But this election (2017) has been marred by pockets of violence, malfeasance, and even the attempted kidnapping of newly elected MPs." —Jonathan Pryke, Australian Broadcasting Corporation

PARLIAMENT

The National Parliament is the top rung within the three-tier government system—national, provincial, and local—similar to that of Australia. The parliament predates Papua New Guinea's independence by eleven years; it was founded in 1964 as the House Assembly of Papua New Guinea. Elections are held not more than five years apart. Citizens over the age of eighteen are eligible to vote and stand for office in the 111-member parliament and in the provincial and local assemblies.

The National Parliament holds ultimate authority over the provincial and local governments. Parliament can vote to veto provincial or local laws that it decides are not in the best interests of the country. It can also suspend those governments in cases of gross mismanagement. The constitution can be altered only by the National Parliament in two votes of seventy-two or more

The local councils represent the most fundamental level of government. More than three hundred councils preside over issues of regional concern. The councils are responsible for the maintenance of roads, bridges, and markets; the provision of fresh water, sanitation, and public transportation services; and the smooth operation of airfields and postal and other communications in isolated areas. Funding comes from registration fees on items like bicycles and dogs, and from taxes levied on land ownership and wages.

members, in two sessions held no less than six weeks apart. The National Parliament is housed in Port Moresby, the National Capital District.

THE STRENGTH OF THE PEOPLE

Papua New Guinea's constitution recognizes the importance of involving people at all levels of society in decision-making processes to provide a sense of cohesion. To do so, they began the adoption of provincial and local governments.

Apart from the National Capital District, which is Port Moresby, and the autonomous region of Bougainville, there are twenty provinces throughout the country. Since 1995, each provincial government has been presided over by the members of the National Parliament from that region, as well as other local officials. The twenty provinces are Central, Chimbu, Eastern Highlands, East New Britain, East Sepik, Enga, Gulf, Hela, Jiwaka, Madang, Manus, Milne Bay, Morobe, New Ireland, Northern, Southern Highlands, Western, Western Highlands, West New Britain, West Sepik.

The provincial governments work with the lower-level local councils on developing plans and budgets for addressing regional issues, including social, health, and educational matters. On the national level, the provincial governments are supported by the Department of Provincial and Local Government Affairs, headed by the minister of inter-government relations, a member of the prime minister's cabinet.

The system of decentralized provincial government was introduced in 1976 to quell secessionist uprisings on some of the islands.

MODERN TRIBAL CONFLICT

The age-old custom of intertribal fighting and the seeking of vengeance still takes place. The Australian government warns travelers that "disputes can quickly escalate into violent clashes and can result in the widespread destruction of property, disruption of normal services and serious injury." Although warriors who kill in tribal warfare can be tried in a court of law, a village will not necessarily cooperate in the arrest of one of its members. This sort of interaction is an excellent example of the juxtaposition between tribal tradition and more westernized government. Tribal custom does not regard this as a breakdown of order but the process by which the customary rules of law and order are implemented. As long as a man's action does not affect his own village adversely, his community usually does not regard it as wrong or deserving of punishment.

JUDICIAL PROCESS

The judicial system of Papua New Guinea is similar to the US and Australian models. A judge decides the outcome of a case after hearing legal representation from both sides, while more serious crimes are brought before a jury. There are several levels in the court system. The Supreme Court is the country's highest court and the final court of appeal, having the authority to interpret and enforce the constitution. Usually three judges sit together during a hearing in this court. The National Court has unlimited jurisdiction, involving a single judge sitting for each hearing. District courts and local courts have more limited powers and are presided over by full-time magistrates. The village courts hear cases such as robbery or assault within the village. The villagers choose their magistrates, who are not required to have legal qualifications.

Other elements of the judicial system include land courts, which settle disputes over traditional landownership, and administrative bodies that control the appointment of judges and magistrates. The discretionary use of the death penalty was reintroduced in 1991 for crimes of rape or murder; however, no one has been executed since 1957. The death penalty was briefly expanded to cover other heavy crimes in 2014, at the same time that punishments for other offenses were updated. In 2016, however, Prime Minister Peter O'Neill put the reforms on hold indefinitely, before any executions were carried out.

Courts face the further challenge of illiterate participants, including many who speak mutually incomprehensible languages. The provision of interpreters and audio recordings of procedures means that more people can

PRIME MINISTERS SINCE INDEPENDENCE

1975	Sir Michael Somare (Pangu Pati)
1980	Sir Julius Chan (People's Progress Party)
1982	Sir Michael Somare (Pangu Pati)
1985	Paias Wingti (People's Democratic Movement)
1988	Sir Rabbie Namaliu (Pangu Pati)
1992	Paias Wingti (People's Democratic Movement)
1994	Sir Julius Chan (People's Progress Party)
1997	Bill Skate (People's National Congress)
1999	Sir Mekere Morauta (People's Democratic Movement)
2002	Sir Michael Somare (National Alliance Party)
2007	Sir Michael Somare (National Alliance Party)
2012	Peter O'Neill (People's National Congress)
2017	Peter O'Neill (People's National Congress)

be engaged in the legal and political operation of their community.

AN EVER-CHANGING GOVERNMENT

From independence until 2002, candidates were elected on a first-past-the-post system, meaning that the person who received the most votes was elected, even with as little as 15 percent of the votes. This led to claims of corruption and bias, and dissatisfaction sometimes spilled over into post-election violence. Few members had continuing popular support for more than one term in parliament, and the high turnover of politicians resulted in a dearth of experience and continuity. National elections are now run on a limited preferential voting system. Voters select their first, second, and third

Peter O'Neill, Papua New Guinea's prime minister, speaks in front of the United Nations General Assembly in New York City in September 2017.

choices, and the first-choice votes are counted. If there is no clear majority, the candidate with the least votes is eliminated, and the votes from those ballot sheets are redistributed according to the voters' second choices. The votes are counted again. This process is repeated until there is a clear majority. This system was first used in 2007.

Unlike in the US and Australian systems, the candidates do not stand for election on an ideological platform but instead rely on their personality and regional ties to secure votes. Once in parliament, they decide which alliance or party they want to support. The politicians are free to change their party allegiance at any time, depending on the issue being debated

In 2016, Papua New Guinea was ranked as one of the most corrupt nations in the world by Transparency International. With allegations of corruption all the way up to the prime minister of the state, it is not surprising that political unrest is found. Human Rights Watch states that "the Papua New Guinean government has failed to adequately address gender inequality, violence, corruption, or excessive use of force by the police." An example of this can be found in Prime Minister Peter O'Neill's first five years in office. Student protests broke out in regards to allegations against O'Neill that included misuse of government funds. The protests went on for months, with oppositionists claiming that the nation deserved greater transparency in government from its politicians and leaders. The protests resulted in a no-confidence vote in 2016. O'Neill won the vote and remained in office, but not without continued discontent from members of the populace.

and the charisma of the main proponents. In trying to achieve a majority vote on any issue, each party attempts to lure members into its camp, and much of a politician's time is spent in political maneuvering, forming and breaking alliances. The drawback is that the shifting alliances of party members can cause instability. With a large and current concern in the nation being the economy and corruption in government, this inconsistency can be problematic. A 2001 law attempted to stabilize the political system by making it more difficult for politicians to switch parties, but much of the law was overturned by the courts.

The prime minister is elected by majority vote in parliament and is usually the chosen leader of the majority party or coalition—an alliance formed by mutual agreement between two or more groups with different interests. There is remarkable ideological consensus among the political parties, with only the best means to the end being debated. However, the continually shifting web of alliances means that any prime minister committed to reform is unable to make tough measures if he or she wishes to remain in power.

The Papua New Guinea Defense Force marches in Papua New Guinea in 1990.

Changes in legislation do not necessarily affect the ruling government's policies, and the National Parliament can challenge the government with a vote of no confidence. Fortunately, the government is protected from such a motion for the first eighteen months after a general election. This time frame was formerly six months, but the rapid changing of governments meant that very little could be achieved by any leader. While this highlights the inefficiency of the system, it also means that no political group in the country is powerful enough to stage a national military coup.

A STANDING MILITARY

The Papua New Guinea Defence Force was created in 1973 while operating under the auspices of the Australian Defence Force. When its command was internalized in Papua New Guinea in 1975, it was merged into a single unified force. It does not have separate army, navy, and air forces but consists of three distinct operational elements: land, maritime, and air.

Within the country the Defence Force patrols the border with Indonesia to prevent border crossings by rebels. Its external involvement arose in 1980 when it was deployed to put down a secessionist movement on Espiritu Santo, an island in the southwest Pacific. On more than one occasion, it was used alongside the Papua New Guinea police force to maintain control during local uprisings, such as the insurrection movement on Bougainville and when civil unrest arose in Port Moresby in 1997 because of political tensions. In the wake of increasing terror in the Asia-Pacific region since the September 11, 2001, attacks in the United States, the Defence Force has increased vigilance to protect the nation. The current roles of this force include but are not limited to border security, maritime surveillance, disaster relief, and maintaining public order.

INTERNET LINKS

http://thecommonwealth.org/our-member-countries/papua-new-guinea/constitution-politics
This website describes the Papua New Guinea commonwealth structure as it currently stands.

http://www.pngembassy.org/government.html
This is the website of Papua New Guinea's embassy in the United States.

ECONOMY

Many Papua New Guineans survive off of small subsistence farms, such as the one depicted here. A variety of foods are grown and harvested for individual and family use.

4

P APUA NEW GUINEA'S ECONOMY is complex. Although overall unemployment is at 2.5 percent, there are higher rates of unemployment in urban areas and more rural locales. Eighty-five percent of people make their living through farming and selling or bartering surplus.

A 2017 Heritage Foundation report describes the economy as "divided between a formal sector based on exports of natural resources and a large informal sector that relies on subsistence farming and other small-scale economic activity." Cash is rising in importance for buying commodities like clothes, beer, tobacco, rice, and canned fish; for education; and for paying taxes. There will need to be an increase in industry and wage-earning jobs in order to support the ever-growing population. In 2017, a majority of wage earners were employed in government agencies and services (about 20 percent), mining, service industries, agriculture, and some manufacturing. These industries have led to exports like oil, gold, copper, timber, palm oil, coffee, and cocoa. With the increased participation in global markets, a formal open market will help the government expand revenue and provide jobs.

A LAND OF RICHES

Papua New Guinea's hopes of economic development rest on its vast resources of minerals, oil, and natural gas. Mining contributes more than a third of the government's tax revenue, and recent expansion in oil and natural gas projects, along with a boom in world resource prices,

> "The country's economy remains dominated by two sectors: the agricultural, forestry, and fishing sector, which engages most of the labor force (the majority informally); and the minerals and energy extraction sector, which accounts for the majority of export earnings and Gross Domestic Product."
> —The World Bank

The minimum wage is low at 3.20 kina per hour, and 39.9 percent of the population lives below the poverty line and cannot meet their material needs. Only 20.3 percent of the population has access to electricity. As a whole, Papua New Guinea is not a wealthy nation, and the economy is a point of contention.

has resulted in significant growth in the economy. Gold, copper, and oil compete as the country's biggest earners, depending on fluctuations in world commodity markets. They equal nearly two-thirds of the nation's export earnings. Oil, natural gas, palm oil, cocoa, crayfish and prawns, logging, and minerals are the targets for extensive exploration and revenue gains.

FROM THE MINES

Papua New Guinea law provides for 5 percent of a mine's gross export sales to be paid in royalties, 20 percent of which goes to the traditional landowners and the remainder to the national government. This gives the provincial

Miners use pans and shovels to find gold in the dirt and rock of Mount Kare.

government a grant from national revenue. Fuels and mining provide 41 percent of the gross domestic product (GDP) of the country. Furthermore, the landowners are provided with equity in the mining company, and compensation is paid to them according to a set schedule. This is based on the area of land affected, the number of trees cut, the amount of gardens destroyed, and the number of fish and other wildlife driven away as a result of mining activities. In addition, the mine is usually required to offer contracts for spin-off businesses to the local people.

Each mine must negotiate other agreements in a forum, and proposals concerning the relocation of housing or education near a mine must be agreed upon before mining can proceed. Despite this often laborious process, ongoing mining operations can cause much dissatisfaction that spills over into civil unrest. An example of this is the continued dumping of toxic waste from the Ok Tedi mine into the Fly River and the resulting environmental degradation.

CONSUMPTION AND DEFORESTATION

Fishing has always been a significant activity in Papua New Guinea, which has 3,201 miles (5,152 km) of coastline, large rivers, and more than six hundred islands. Fishing is carried out mainly by coastal villagers using traditional methods, a few foreign trawlers licensed to fish in the waters, and a fleet of tuna boats. The tropical waters support a variety of fish including tuna, Spanish mackerel, and barramundi. The canneries in Lae work predominantly in tuna and have made the city Papua New Guinea's main manufacturing location. The Oxford Business Group estimates that between 12 and 17 percent of the world's tuna supply, including slapjack and yellowfin, is caught within the waters of Papua New Guinea.

Forestry has been active in Papua New Guinea since before independence. Inadequate laws and lack of monitoring by authorities have resulted in virgin rain forests being torn apart with little regard for environmental conservation. Such destruction resulted in land erosion, rivers choked with silt, and wildlife loss. It also affected the rural people who use forest resources for building, food, and medicine. Nonetheless, forestry has long

been an export earner, with a large variety of high-quality hardwoods being harvested. The Australian Broadcasting Corporation reports that 4,423 square miles (11,457 sq km) of previously untouched forest was harmed by logging and other activity between 2002 and 2014. With that, Papua New Guinea became the second-largest producer of tropical hardwoods.

Clearing rain forests such as this one in Southern Highlands province is decimating the country's biodiversity and ecological treasures.

A DEVELOPING NATION

Manufacturing needs further development despite the government's attempts to promote expansion. Deterrents to growth include a largely unskilled labor force, a lack of vocational training facilities, low productivity, limited cash resources in the economy, a limited local market to sell to, and competition against cheap imports (because of the strength of the Papua New Guinea currency, the kina, against external markets). The Investment Promotion Authority acknowledges that "currently, Papua New Guinea imports most processed food, clothing and footwear and most of the inputs to industry and commerce." In 2012, manufacturing accounted for only 6.2 percent of the country's export revenue.

The isolation of many communities means that the high cost of transporting goods to their area outweighs the local desire to possess them. One area of concern is the country's dependence on imported food. Papua New Guinea imports a huge portion of its grains, specifically three-quarters of the rice consumed, and almost all of its processed foods, but there is a push to produce more of its own food, and funding for domestic rice growers is available.

Some processing of exported agricultural items such as coffee, palm oil, and timber takes place, and there are a few clothing and metal fabrication factories. Beer, cigarettes, and soft drinks have been produced in the country since before independence, and the sugar industry was developed in the early 1980s. To protect the local sugar industry, sugar imports, once banned, are heavily taxed. Papua New Guinea is self-sufficient in chicken and chicken-based products, and meat canneries have been established in Madang and Port Moresby, but these do not singlehandedly sustain the protein requirements

This image shows a store in downtown Lae.

of the whole country. The canneries in Lae help add to the production and manufacturing, as well as support protein requirements. That said, some areas no longer have the forest resources to support protein supplies, and people in some communities cannot afford to buy canned meat.

AGRICULTURE

As well as creating a livelihood for 85 percent of the population, agriculture plays a very important part in the economy. It provides 23.8 percent of exports and makes up 22.3 percent of the GDP. There are two distinct types of farming: subsistence farming, the small-scale cultivation of food for sale in the markets, and cash cropping. Subsistence farming means that a family grows only enough food to feed itself. Cash cropping is the cultivation of crops such as coffee and palm oil for sale.

Papua New Guinean farmers have a strong subsistence base with diversified crops to avoid shortages in times of blight or economic struggle. Many villagers move in and out of cash cropping when they have a need for income and return to subsistence farming when that need is met. Village root crops (sweet potatoes, yams, and taros) grow quickly and produce a high yield of food energy for the amount of work put into their cultivation.

Arabica coffee beans, such as those produced by the Tramar Group, are one of the profitable cash crops grown in the fertile soils of Papua New Guinea.

Therefore, time and energy can be devoted to other crops or income-generating activities. Selling handmade items and extra crops brings in additional income.

AGRICULTURAL EXPORTS AND GLOBAL TRADE

Coffee, palm oil, and cocoa are the most important cash crops. Copra, the dried flesh of the coconut that coconut oil is extracted from, was a major economic contributor for many years, but decline in the world commodity market rendered its production unrewarding. Since the country's independence in 1975, there has been a dramatic drop in copra output and the number of people employed on coconut plantations. Large palm oil plantations and processing plants are in Northern Province, Milne Bay, and the western part of New Britain. Although tea grown in the highlands is good, it has not met economic expectations and falls behind cocoa and copra as a potential revenue earner. Vanilla also brings in revenue. Rubber production is continuing as well.

International trade in Papua New Guinea has seen an upswing since 2014 when ExxonMobil completed a $19 billion project for harvesting underused liquid natural gas beneath the island. With about 5.4 trillion cubic feet (155 billion cubic meters) of unused natural gas, this could be a high revenue yield in the future, as well as a way to draw foreign investors to the country. Since the success of the project, other similar companies have shown interest in developing in Papua New Guinea. Total S.A., a large French company with interests in fuel and gas, is planning a similar project on the island with expectations of completion by 2020.

ECOTOURISM

Ecotourism is rising in popularity in Papua New Guinea. The beauty of the land and reefs around the islands draws tourists, conservationists, and wildlife enthusiasts. Hiking the Kokoda Trail allows travelers to visit the site of the Kokoda battle during World War II as well as see the rich beauty of the landscape. Wildlife enthusiasts can bird-watch in the jungles as an array of different birds of paradise find their home on the islands. For the marine farers, diving off of Kimbe Bay is a stunning experience, with more than 860 species of fish and 413 species of coral. The richness and beauty of the land draw tourists and revenue, and the government is encouraging the growth of this industry. The hope is that ecotourism will bring in new streams of revenue and thereby decrease environmental impact from other industries.

INTERNET LINKS

https://www.pwc.com/pg/en/industries/industries-agriculture-and-fisheries.html
This website details Papua New Guinea's agriculture and fisheries industries today.

https://ramumine.wordpress.com
This blog examines different issues concerning the mines of Papua New Guinea.

http://documents.worldbank.org/curated/en/333681479824448362/pdf/SFG2662-EA-P158807-Box396334B-PUBLIC-Disclosed-11-21-2016.pdf
This is a comprehensive look at Papua New Guinea's goals for tourism expansion in the coming years.

ENVIRONMENT

The diverse landscapes of Papua New Guinea are breathtaking and varied, with such rich jungle vegetation and beautiful coves as found here in Rabaul on New Britain Island in the Bismark Archipelago.

5

PAPUA NEW GUINEA IS WORKING on conservation efforts. Extensive logging, mining, and exploitation of natural resources led to significant forest depreciation. There is an increase in pollution and erosion, which further endangers animals.

In the twenty-first century, the government and other private organizations have worked to make strides toward conservation and preservation. Organizations like the Nature Conservancy, whose mission is "empowering local people to design sustainable futures for the lands and waters that surround them," are working with locals to encourage and teach conservation. Industrialization comes with waste, but conservationists do not want it to come at the cost of the incredible landscape and fauna of the region. Geographic isolation and island status has created many diverse animal and plant species to be protected. The resulting biodiversity is outstanding and one of the greatest treasures of Papua New Guinea.

GLOBAL WARMING

Due to its limited manufacturing sector, Papua New Guinea uses few carbon fuels. According to the Global Carbon Atlas, the country generated 7.3 million tons (6.6 million metric tons) of carbon dioxide emissions in 2015 due to the burning of fossil fuels. This is a small number compared with the 5,968 million tons (5,414 million metric tons) generated in the United States in 2015. However, removal of forests is another source

Some of the massive destruction caused by global warming is easily visible in the bleached coral off the coast of New Ireland, Papua New Guinea.

of greenhouse gases, accounting for a significant percentage of the world's heat-trapping gases each year. Given the deforestation rates in Papua New Guinea, this poses a much more significant environmental threat in the country than the burning of fossil fuels. REDD Desk estimates that deforestation and other land-use issues in Papua New Guinea accounted for 121 to 139 million tons (110—126 million metric tons) of carbon dioxide emissions in 2010. These gases are believed to be adding to the warming effect in Earth's atmosphere, leading to widespread environmental change.

Global warming is affecting the island of New Guinea. In 2006, scientists visiting the Puncak Jaya area in the western central highlands of New Guinea observed that the equatorial glacier there was melting at a rate that suggested the area was warming at twice the global rate, probably due to its altitude. Areas like the East Sepik region are very prone to flooding. Rising sea levels are also affecting parts of the country. These can have huge impacts on local and global communities.

Efforts began in 2014 to educate locals on the value of preserving mangrove trees, which protect against erosion and land loss caused by rising waters. Further damage will continue to be evident, but efforts are being made to slow and stop the effects.

The nation, in accordance with the United Nations Development Programme, has also launched the Protected Area Policy, which allows communities to sustainably fund conservation efforts in forest, marine, and coastal areas. In areas like New Britain, efforts are being made to help locals that depend on forest degradation and logging practices for subsistence by helping them develop other industries like ecotourism and sustainable farming methods not based on logging. Forest protection decreases greenhouse emissions because extensive vegetation recycles damaging

In the lowlands near the Rams River is Wanang, a small village with a large goal. When the area was set to be logged, ten local village clans banded together to form the Wanang Conservation Area. It would protect the 24,700-acre (10,000-hectare) rain forest from the logging industry. Their efforts preserved the habit of "more than 550 species of trees and shrubs, and 142 species of birds, 200 species of butterflies and thousand[s] of other plants and species." In 2015, the region was granted the prestigious UN Development Programme Equator Prize, which recognizes community-based and natural, sustainable solutions to developmental problems.

greenhouse gases through their basic life processes and photosynthesis. By protecting forests, Papua New Guineans are protecting the world's atmosphere.

THE RUN OFF

Mining has been a major source of income for Papua New Guinea for a century, but huge open-cut mines have caused widespread environmental damage. The construction of roads, mining camps, processing facilities, and the open-cut mines themselves disturb pristine wilderness. The impact is usually felt for several miles around the mine sites because Papua New Guinean mines do not use tailings dams—embankments to contain the waste products and excess fluid. Instead, the mines discharge their crushed and chemically treated ore wastes directly into rivers and offshore waters. These "tailings" contain at least 50 percent sedimentation, processing chemicals, and other toxic substances like heavy metals. These chemicals poison aquatic species and gradually become more concentrated in the food chain, including traditional village foods. The effects are felt downstream all the way to coastal waters, where corals are particularly vulnerable to them. The Panguna mine in Bougainville, now closed, and the Ok Tedi mine in the Star Mountains in Western Province are two examples of the terrible impact this pollution has in Papua New Guinea.

TROUBLE WITH THE OK TEDI MINE

One of the most controversial mines in Papua New Guinea, the Ok Tedi Mine, holds a place in the country's recent past. In the 1980s, a tailings dam designed to remove tailings before releasing wastewater was originally planned for the Ok Tedi copper and gold mine in Western Province, but it was abandoned after an earthquake in 1984 revealed how geologically unstable the area was. The government subsequently allowed the mine to go ahead without the dam. From 1984 to 2001, each year an average of 90 million tons (82 million metric tons) of waste and wastewater was released into the Ok Tedi River and flowed downstream into the Fly River system, polluting them with arsenic and toxic heavy metals.

Ok Tedi Mining Limited reported that the water was of drinkable quality and aquatic life was not affected, but evidence said otherwise. The sago swamps and riverside gardens died off, and hunted pigs and deer emitted a smell that made them inedible. Furthermore, the World Wildlife Fund reported that "Ok Tedi's reports revealed that fish stocks in the upper Ok Tedi had declined by 50 [percent] to 80 [percent] from the pre-mining levels." People experienced skin diseases and stomach problems from drinking the water. Meanwhile, flooding from sedimentation ruined houses and destroyed trees.

The damage led to lawsuits against BHP Billiton, which owned the majority of the mine, and resulted in the company settling out of court to the tune of $28.6 million in damages and an agreement to dredge the rivers. In order to continue mine operations into the year 2025, the mine paid out 15 million kina ($4.7 million US) in April 2016 to affected communities.

FOREST LOSS

Logging is a significant income source in Papua New Guinea, but it also causes the vast majority of the country's carbon dioxide emissions. Of the nation's nearly 90 million acres (36 million ha) of forest, about 2.8 million acres (1.1 million ha) were cleared between 2002 and 2014. With concern for the future, the conversation turned toward conservation and sustainability. Although the government developed tighter forestry regulations in the early 1990s aimed at creating sustainable practices, they are difficult to police in remote areas.

Forests are also cleared for farming and housing, particularly as the population grows and more land is needed for farming. Furthermore, global interest in growing crops cheaply for the production of biofuel placed increased pressure on forests in developing countries like Papua New Guinea. The use of fire to rapidly clear land sometimes causes widespread forest fires. Deforestation causes habitat damage, soil erosion and nutrient loss, pollution of waterways, and loss of wildlife corridors, which further endangers native animals and allows the introduction of invasive species into previously undisturbed areas. Removal of woodland can also limit traditional hunting and farming practices, leading to culture loss. Along with old-growth forest destruction, logging operations damage the wilderness areas, causing soil erosion along timber roads and camps and leading to the dumping of industrial and camp wastes and raw effluence.

Logging, such as that completed here on New Britain in Papua New Guinea, is a huge source of revenue but also destroys rich ecological diversity.

PAPUA NEW GUINEA AND THE PARIS CLIMATE AGREEMENT

Papua New Guinea is an active participant in the Paris Climate Agreement, a 2016 international agreement to fight climate change and to avoid having Earth's temperature rise in the face of pollution and greenhouse gas emissions. In March 2016, Papua New Guinea became the first nation to submit their finalized Nationally Determined Contribution plan to the United Nation. This plan is the national climate action plan designed to help the nation transfer to 100 percent renewable energy by 2030.

IMPACT ON THE LAND AND WATER

Removal of vegetation from logging and farming, coupled with high rainfall, destabilizes soil and results in a high rate of erosion by wind and rain. Valuable nutrient-rich topsoil is washed away, leaving poorer, dustier, and drier soil behind. The silt ends up in watercourses, where it affects downstream ecosystems by blocking the light needed by algae and other water plants. It also alters the balance of nutrients in the water. This harms species of aquatic animals and has a flow-on effect in rivers, coastal floodplains, and marine waters, including coastal fish-hatchery areas and fishing areas.

CONSERVATION AND WILDLIFE

The Goodfellow's tree kangaroo is an endangered animal found in the forests of Papua New Guinea.

Between 5 and 7 percent of the world's total number of species are believed to be found in Papua New Guinea, with over twenty thousand species of flowering plants alone. Cool Earth says that "scientists estimate that more than half the plants and animals found in Papua New Guinea have yet to be named." With more than two hundred thousand known species, this shows the cornucopia of wildlife that exists on the islands. Exploration of the islands' diversity is continuous, with new discoveries made as recently as 2017. Many of these species are rare and only inhabit small areas. There are also many endangered species living in the country.

Along with habitat loss due to logging, mining, and agriculture, more animals are being killed through traditional hunting and fishing for needed protein as the population swells. Among the critically endangered species are sawfish, the leatherback and hawksbill turtles, three types of bat, two species of water rats, and two types of mice. Other endangered mammals include the Alpine wallaby, the Fergusson Island striped possum, the Goodfellow's tree kangaroo, the black-spotted cuscus, and the long-beaked echidna.

About fifty-two species of endangered animals have been declared national animals by the Papua New Guinea government. National animals are protected by law and can only be killed in traditional manners for customary uses. They cannot be bought, sold, kept, or exported. They include all thirty-three types of birds of paradise as well as several other types of birds, all seven species of birdwing butterflies, the long-beaked echidna, the dugong, the tree kangaroo, and the Boelen's python.

TRASH AND WASTE

In traditional life, everything that the villagers used was sourced from their surroundings and could be discarded back into the environment, burned, or left to rot in a pile. These practices do not work with modern non-biodegradable materials such as food packaging, and waste management remains an issue in Papua New Guinea. In urban areas, contractors remove unsorted household and industrial waste to landfill dumps, where it is haphazardly burned or buried. Some householders burn or bury their own garbage, while others leave it in piles.

A certain amount of de facto recycling—sale or reuse of discarded items such as clothes, building materials, furniture, and household goods—takes place in areas where cash is scarce. There are commercial scrap-metal recyclers in the urban centers, and people collect aluminum cans and glass bottles for the small fee that these companies pay. Recycling does not extend to paper or plastics, and plastic waste is problematic. Plastic bags and packaging are commonly discarded, often finding their way into waterways, or are burned, releasing toxic gases.

A pile of trash fills the street in a market, showing the trouble arising from modern refuse.

Papua New Guinea is struggling to find clean water as well. Due to poor waste management, 60 percent of the population does not have access to safe drinking water. The Water Supply and Sanitation Development Plan was initiated in 2015 to help combat this huge deficit.

CONSERVATION

The government of Papua New Guinea committed the country to the principles of conservation and environmental sustainability when it ratified the United Nations Convention on Biological Diversity in 1993 and again in 2016 with the Paris Climate Agreement. The Department of Environment and Conservation is responsible for protecting Papua New Guinea's natural resources, and it administers legislation covering national parks, protection and controlled farming, environmental planning, regulating hazardous materials, and managing water resources.

The bulk of conservation work is done by internationally funded nongovernmental organizations that work with local communities to ensure success. They work primarily with small, local groups to create awareness of environmental issues and teach people how to preserve their local resources. They encourage ecologically sound practices and the development of sustainable sources of income, such as village-based logging using portable sawmills referred to as "wokabaut" sawmills, ecotourism, insect farming, sustainable deepwater fishing, artifact production, and small-scale organic farming. They are politically and legally active, lobbying to stop further destruction of the environment, particularly by large mining and logging companies.

FINDING WAYS TO EMBRACE RENEWABLE RESOURCES

The government took great strides toward preservation and conservation with the Visions 2050 plan and the National Strategic Plan 2010—2030. The Visions 2050 plan was set in place to help the nation reach the goal of being in the top fifty of the United Nations Human Development Index by 2050. A portion of the plan includes finding environmentally sustainable methods and hindering climate change, as well as participating in large-scale government planning for the development of all sectors of society to foster a happier, healthier, and more sustainable society within Papua New Guinea. The National Strategic Plan 2010—2030 is a component of the grand arching Visions 2050 plan. The plan dictates greater education of the people of Papua New Guinea on climate change and sustainable practices, as well as establishing an Institute of Environmental Sustainability and Climate Change to formalize knowledge. This will help with climate change initiatives and sustainable practices. Part of these initiatives will work with sustainable energy sources like hydro and solar power. An example of such a project is the Karimui dam being built in Chimbu Province. When completed in 2023, it will provide 1,800 megawatts of power. With projects like this, the nation plans to have at least 32 percent of its power be fully renewable by 2030. Ultimately, they hope to use 100 percent renewable energy by the year 2050.

INTERNET LINKS

http://www.earthsendangered.com/search-regions3.asp?search=1&sgroup=allgroups&ID=283
This list lets you explore endangered animals by region and locale.

http://www.globalcarbonatlas.org/en/CO2-emissions
This is a link to an interactive map that shows different levels of CO_2 emissions by nation.

https://www.nature.org/ourinitiatives/regions/asiaandthepacific/papuanewguinea/index.htm
The Nature Conservancy works with local communities in Papua New Guinea on conservation and green initiatives.

PAPUA NEW GUINEANS

Men from a tribe in Paiya, Western Highlands Province, dance and sing while wearing brightly colored clothing, accessories, and body paint at a sing-sing.

6

THE PEOPLE OF PAPUA NEW Guinea are as unique and diverse as the country's landscape. They are "unique, complex, and full of contradictions." The racial origins are Papuan, Melanesian, Micronesian, and Polynesian. Race, however, is not the dividing force between cultures in Papua New Guinea. Clan ties and family lines define inclusion far more than race. Tribe and clan affiliations are often a part of a person's identity.

A CHANGING POPULATION

In 2017, the population was estimated to be about 8 million people, but it is growing quickly. This sudden rise indicates improved national health conditions and the absence of birth control. The rapid population explosion will exert enormous pressure on health and education services, housing, and national resources.

The country's population is young, with 33.4 percent under the age of 14, and 53.3 percent under the age of 25. The life expectancy remains low at 65 years for males and 69.5 years for females. The average fertility rate is quite high, at about 3 births for each childbearing woman.

"Today there are over seven million people living in Papua New Guinea—more than a third of them in the rugged Highlands. The traditional Melanesian cultures are kept alive in elaborate rituals that accompany deaths, feasts, marriages, compensation ceremonies and initiation rites."
—Papua New Guinea: A Million Different Journeys website

The death rate stands at 6.5 deaths per 1,000 people; the world average is 7.8 deaths per 1,000.

New challenges arise with an increasing population. There is potential for food shortages and pressures on an environment that has never supported so many people. Furthermore, more people means an increased chance for interpersonal clashes. Max Kep, the director of the Papua New Guinea national Office of Urbanization, stated in 2011, "Without doubt, rapid population growth is adding to the risk of conflict." Tribal conflict continues today, and rising pressure from a growing population could fuel that fire with land shortages and competition over resources.

FAMILY AND GIVING

Family, clan, and tribe are the essential social units. A household may share its food, home, labor, land, or pigs with a family member or someone from the same tribe whether the relation is close or distant. This is in accordance

Two mothers and their children sit outside a house in the highlands of Papua New Guinea.

Village elders, called "big men," are political and social figureheads. They are often wealthy by Papua New Guinean standards. These big men usually have multiple wives to help them with the housework, raising of pigs, and gardening. A person's social power has, historically, been determined by how much a person can afford to give away to others.

with the Melanesian concept of *wantok* (WAN-tohk), which acts as a social security network. A system of reciprocity means that something will usually be given in return—perhaps loyalty in conflict or help at a later date. *Wantok* is considered "the glue that binds the nation together" because it helps ensure the health and wellness of the tribe and the individual.

Property, a prerequisite of wealth, does not always belong to the individual here. In some instances, land and jewelry are owned by the whole clan or tribe and distributed according to a complex network of ties. Ownership is often vested in the household, which is usually headed by a male. Wealth is determined not just by the things one has but also by how much one gives away to others.

The village elders, or "big men," display their affluence by giving wealth away. This in return provides them with a great deal of influence because villagers are then indebted to them. Big men do the heavy negotiating, settle disputes, and plan when to slaughter the pigs. An elaborate system of negotiation, trading ceremonies, and ritualized battles exists among clans throughout the country to preserve or restore order.

FASHION

Western-style clothes are common in the urban areas and are increasingly popular in rural areas, particularly around Christian missions. They tend to be casual and geared toward the tropical climate. The women wear simple dresses or skirts and blouses, while the men wear shorts with a shirt, though in the rural areas the shirts are dispensable. Traditional clothing remains the norm for some tribes in the more remote areas, where Western-style

clothing is not accessible, and it is commonly worn for special events throughout the country.

Fashion shows the close relationship people have with the environment through vibrant hues and ornate clothes. Feathers, bones, leaves, seeds, shells, and natural pigments are the basis for dress. Often such finery has symbolic meanings—it represents the qualities of the wearer or the individual's status or is a symbol of myths and customs revered by the tribe.

In Papua New Guinea, the native clothes are adorned with decorations and often are works of art. The bright plumage of birds of paradise and other types of feathers are woven into elaborate headdresses for the men. These are then decorated with valuable shells and animal teeth. Several groups, such as the Huli and the Komblo in the highlands, weave huge wigs from human hair and burrs, then decorate them with paints, dried flowers, and even iridescent beetles. The highlanders in particular favor nose piercing.

The septum, the fleshy wall between the two nostrils, is pierced with a sharp piece of wood, bone, or cassowary quill, and any variety of impressive objects are placed through the hole, including boar tusks, cassowary quills or bones, long dried grasses, or shells.

Loincloths, or *laplaps* (LAP-laps), tend to resemble aprons, with a longer section of cloth or strands of woven cords and leaves worn at the front and a smaller bunch of leaves tucked into the waistband behind. Males of several tribes near the western border wear penis gourds and little else. The gourds are long marrowlike fruit, up to 3 feet (0.9 meters) in length. These are dried, cut open, and worn over the penis and tied to the waist with string. Cassowary bones, daggers, and tools are tucked into woven armbands and leg bands. Sometimes ritual scar designs are cut into the flesh at a boy's coming-of-age ceremony, especially among those living along the Sepik River, where the designs represent the claw marks of crocodiles.

Face painting, facial tattoos, and other body adornments and modifications are common. Here, a young Korafe tribe member's face is painted in Cape Nelson, Tufi, Papua New Guinea.

This young girl uses a *bilum* to carry around her baby sister.

The painting of faces, bodies, and hair is practiced by both genders, traditionally with charcoal and pigments, though modern paints are now favored, especially for ceremonies, for their brightness. In some areas, both men and women rub their skins with a variety of leaves and oils like pig fat to leave an attractive sheen.

WOMEN'S STYLE

Women's traditional dress is colorful but less elaborate than men's. It is customary in some areas for women to wear tattoos on the face. The tattoos are made in a painful process, using just a needle and charcoal. Lines of dots in the shapes of suns, stars, and arrows, as well as curved parallel lines, decorate the face.

Women in most areas traditionally wear plain grass or simple skirts and are sometimes bare breasted. In some regions, unwed girls modestly cover themselves with a small woven patch of fabric. Strings of beads, leaves, feathers, and teeth are worn in abundance during ceremonial occasions. Headdresses are for special events but tend to be smaller and less ornate than those of the men. Huge woven bags called *bilums* (BILL-uhms),

VIOLENCE AGAINST WOMEN

Papua New Guinea is faced with a very real problem. There are high rates of violence and domestic abuse against women. In 2015, it was reported that two-thirds of women in Papua New Guinea suffer domestic abuse. The rates of violence in Papua New Guinea are usually only seen in war-torn conflict zones. Though the country passed a family protection bill in 2013 that made such violence illegal, high rates of domestic abuse are still seen. In 2016, Huffington Post *called Papua New Guinea "one of the most dangerous countries in the world to be a woman."*

made of bark fiber or nylon, are used to carry everything from babies to firewood, with the strap placed on the head to support the weight of the load falling behind.

SHOWING GRIEF

In several areas, women in mourning wear numerous loops of grass seeds that range in color from pale gray to white. These are referred to in English as Job's tears. A full load of these can weigh up to 31 pounds (14 kg). Each day the woman removes one loop. Mourning ends when she takes off the last loop of seeds, usually about nine months after the death of her husband. In some areas, the women coat themselves with a bluish-gray clay while in mourning.

This highland widow is mourning the death of her husband by covering her skin in gray clay and wearing mourning necklaces made of grass seeds.

INTERNET LINKS

http://www.emtv.com.pg/women-and-the-glass-ceiling-in-papua-new-guinea
EMTV.com discusses the struggles women face in the business realm in Papua New Guinea.

https://www.youtube.com/watch?v=cPhzRJU9RNo
This documentary explores women's roles in Papua New Guinea's society.

LIFESTYLE

Men sit by a fire in a *haus tambaran* in the Sepik River region. These areas are popular in Papua New Guinean villages.

PAPUA NEW GUINEA'S DIVERSE landscape ensures diverse lifestyles. Anthropological journalists Iago Corazza and Greta Ropa describe the diversity of the nation as an "extraordinary variety of distinct cultures having separate languages and unique customs." It is an incredibly varied place. Urban centers contain about 13 percent of the population and are much more westernized, with buildings, shopping, and all the other urban conveniences like internet and electricity.

There is insufficient low-cost housing as most of the population is not wealthy. This leads to shantytowns surrounding big cities constructed out of whatever materials can be found. The remainder of the population make their homes in remote villages with traditional housing and fires to keep away mosquitoes. The rural areas are usually less advantaged, with few real roads and problems finding sanitary water sources.

TRIBAL VILLAGES

Outside the towns, most housing is constructed using the resources found in the forests or the swamps, with the occasional addition of industrial materials such as corrugated iron sheets. The structures

7

"I'm constantly surprised by the complexity and cultural diversity of this country. It's like trying to solve a deep mystery, with a surprise always ahead of you. No wonder they call this 'the land of the unexpected.'"
—Karl Galing, World Bank

vary from small huts at ground level with a single room housing an entire family to large communal longhouses accommodating an extended family or segregated groups of men and women.

The houses are arranged in long rows or in circular clusters and may be rectangular or round. The house frame is a strong wooden or bamboo structure, and it is topped with thatched roofs of strong kunai grass, sago palm fronds, or other broad leaves. Wooden or bamboo slats or bark laced together with thin cane strips form the walls. In many areas, houses are built on stilts.

A fire is usually left smoldering in a central hearth of dirt or stones or in a clay bowl. After dark, the fire is often the only source of light in villages with little or limited access to electricity or gas, and smoke keeps away mosquitoes. That smoke escapes through any exit it can, as windows are not desirable in a land that is infested with flying insects, drenched in monsoonal rains, and susceptible to tribal warfare. Inside the house there may be wooden beds, mats, or coarse fiber bedcovers. Food items and other goods are commonly stored in baskets, string bags hung from the rafters, or in unglazed clay pots.

A village clearing is reserved for communal gatherings, and it is typically the women's job to sweep it. Many highland villages have a wide ditch built around them to protect them against attacks and to prevent pigs, chickens, and small children from wandering out into the surrounding wilderness.

WEALTH, KINA, AND KULA

As recently as thirty years ago, some people insisted on being paid only in coins and would not take paper money. People attach more value to traditional wealth than to the national currency. While a large pig may be worth 500—1,000 kina ($156.75—$313.50 US), many people would prefer to own the pig instead of the cash. Likewise, cassowaries and any weapons or jewelry made from parts of this animal are highly sought after.

The national currency is named after the kina shell, a large crescent shape cut from the gold-lipped pearl shell. Kina shells are worn proudly on a length of string threaded between two holes in the shell and are still used in trade and bartering. Occasionally, an individual shell will be given its own name, and the number of knots in its string indicates the number of owners the shell has had. In the highlands, it is common to see long necklaces made of tiny bamboo sticks strung in a ladderlike fashion. Each strip on these *omak* (OH-mak) necklaces represents either ten pigs or ten kina shells given away or lent by the owner, an important indication of social status.

Trade is commonly conducted with nonpaper money. In Milne Bay, business can be conducted with grass skirts or dry bundles of etched banana leaves called *doba* (DOH-bah) for yams and shell valuables. In New Britain, *tambu* (TAHM-boo), tiny shells strung on a piece of bamboo, are used as currency, especially in the markets.

Another kind of trade, deeply rooted in tradition and most popularly carried out on the Trobriand Islands, is called kula. Kula are items, such as shells or necklaces, exchanged between clans and individuals who have a long-established trading partnership. Kula are exchanged following specific trade routes and ceremonial customs. Some kula travel hundreds of miles to be exchanged. Once they are exchanged, whoever possesses the kula earns prestige and can be elevated in rank within a clan. Kula traditions are upheld between families from generation to generation.

NAVIGATING THE COUNTRYSIDE

The fastest and easiest way to travel in Papua New Guinea is by air. The country's development heavily depended on its aviation facilities, and most mineral and forestry exploration takes place with sophisticated equipment transported by air. Many of the airstrips are small and rough, however, and flights often have long waiting lists.

Along the waterways, especially the Sepik River, the dugout canoe is king. The traffic can get quite heavy on the river on market days. Large and midsize freighters and passenger boats provide transportation between the islands, but it may take a couple of days to reach a destination because freight is loaded on or taken off along the way. Villagers make use of their own boats, which include traditional canoes, diesel-run wooden boats, and small dinghies with outboard motors known as speedies or banana boats.

The majority of roads are rough, and travelers can be ambushed by armed robbers. Sometimes heavy rainfall makes roads impassable, muddy bogs.

Nevertheless, they are useful for shorter journeys and for those with little money. People can choose to walk, the road often being the only clearing through dense vegetation, or to take a PMV—a public motor vehicle. A PMV can be just about any vehicle, from a truck with hard benches to a Japanese-made minibus. PMVs travel along predetermined routes through the towns and the countryside. Despite a lack of policing of the roads in the rural areas, the PMVs are quite safe to travel in because the drivers are aware of the stiff fines should they run over even a chicken, let alone if they injure a pedestrian or a passenger.

LAND RIGHTS

About 97 percent of land in Papua New Guinea comes under traditional landownership laws, a contrast to the Western system based on individual, legally documented ownership. Traditional ownership is based on human memory, often held by a community, and is distributed according to a complex web of individual and clan rights. The systems differ from place to place. Disputes between tribes over landownership boundaries used to be cause for warfare, and tensions can still run high today between groups and clans within any single tribe.

Some areas remain communally owned. This becomes a problem when land transfer is required for nontraditional purposes—for example, the sale of land for cash cropping or the establishment of mining rights in a particular area. Different groups may stake their claim on a single piece of land based on each group's oral history, and disputes inevitably arise. Sometimes the wrong people are paid compensation for the use of the land.

LAND OWNERSHIP AND CONFLICT

In Papua New Guinea, everything is owned by someone. Even seemingly remote areas of land have a traditional owner somewhere, and the ownership

of individual animals is known throughout the entire village. If land is to be used, the owners expect immediate and generous compensation or rent. Any damage, whether intended or accidental, to life, limb, or property requires ritual compensation to avert similar violence in return.

The size of tribal communities varies from a few hundred to a few thousand members, and there are often traditional intertribal hostilities. Each tribe or clan is collectively held responsible for the actions of its individual members and actively seeks compensation if one of its members becomes a victim. Failing to make the appropriate payback compensation is a worse crime than the original act, and revenge is accordingly brutal. Tribal war may result when negotiations between clans or tribes fail.

MARRIAGE CONTRACTS

Marriage is less about the individual's ties and more about the wider social relationships that are strengthened through the marriage contract. An essential element is the payment of a "bride price" by the groom to his bride's parents or clan. In certain areas of Papua New Guinea, marriage centers on the final payment of the bride price. The groom and his clan, dressed in their customary finery, walk to the ceremonial clearing where the goods are laid out in front of the bride's clan. Leaf-wrapped kina shells rubbed with red

Between 2015 and 2016, the government began amending marriage laws in Papua New Guinea. The Matrimonial (Clauses) Bill 2015 set the legal age for consent to marriage at eighteen years old. Prior to this edict, child marriage was legal in Papua New Guinea. The new law ensures hefty fines and possible jail time should someone force another person into an underage marriage.

ocher, pigs, cash notes attached to a large display pole, and even cassowaries can form part of this important payment. They are examined by the bride's family, and once the goods are accepted, the marriage is sealed.

These payments are still common, even in the cities, where marriages take place between members of clans from different provinces, and among Christians, too, who are married with a church ceremony. Despite efforts by village councils to control the prices, payments can be high. In the highlands, they can consist of scores of pigs and a small cash payment. In the cities, thousands of kina can change hands, and the sum can rise even higher among wealthy families. This payment is also seen as a deterrent from divorce and seems to send a message to a husband that his wife is his property. This attitude has also led to increases in domestic abuse.

Traditionally, adultery was considered a crime worse than murder. It was seen as an insult to the aggrieved spouse's entire clan and was punishable by death. Today this strict code has relaxed, but adultery is still a very serious offense in some groups.

WOMEN AND WORK

Women are traditionally considered subordinate to men. In a few societies in the New Guinea islands and Milne Bay, property is passed on matrilineally—that is, men inherit property through the female line. For example, a man may inherit goods from his mother's brother. Women in these societies perform the bulk of the subsistence farming, tend pigs, raise children, and prepare food. However, the women are not accorded social or political equality. The men are still custodians of family property, wield power in decision-making, and receive the cash and the choicest cuts of food. Women have little recourse should they disagree with their husbands, fathers, or elders. Many men feel justified in beating their wives or daughters.

Women have set up their own trading networks, shareholding concerns, and educational support systems. This way they are achieving success and reaping monetary and social benefits in both private and public sectors or respected positions in their home communities.

Trade of woven goods, like the baskets these women are making, is one way women can create wealth of their own and earn some independence for themselves.

Paid employment seems the best opportunity to leave traditional subservience, as it allows women to participate in a modern world. That said, it is challenging to work because there is so little protection for women. Sometimes, the danger to women outweighs the financial gain of working. Furthermore, many rural societies still hold negative perceptions about sending their daughters to school. The labor a girl provides in domestic chores is much greater than that of her brother, so in times of financial crisis, the girl is taken out of school before her brother.

Men need women because they are responsible for agricultural production. Having a wife is a requirement for adding to one's wealth. In some areas, the amount of land allotted to a man's family for farming depends on the number of women he has in the household, and polygamy is practiced in many areas to maximize wealth and status. Daughters who marry earn their parents a bride payment that can be quite substantial. The parents may be tempted to choose the union that is most profitable or politically beneficial to themselves ahead of their daughter's needs.

HEALTH CARE FOR A GROWING POPULATION

Today, the health-care system is struggling to keep up with the booming population. Bouts of malaria, tuberculosis, diarrhea, and acute respiratory disease are common, and the country is still facing an HIV epidemic. Rising fear of the Zika virus also affects women, specifically because fetuses are affected during development, though the effects may not be noticed until as late as birth. For women, childbirth carries a further risk, with high maternal mortality rates.

Health services are delivered through a system of small first-aid posts staffed by orderlies with rudimentary medical and hygiene skills and larger health centers with a higher level of expertise. There are also provincial hospitals with trained medical staff, but these are often in urban areas. The Christian churches provide substantial health services in rural areas. They run several hospitals and train many nurses and community health workers. In many areas, people still administer their own healing methods, ranging from medicinal plants to body paint.

Wide-scale mobile vaccination programs have halted the spread of infectious diseases such as measles and yaws, a highly contagious skin disease. Climate and remoteness hamper large-scale health improvements and pose some of the largest challenges the government faces in health care. However, the government launched an improvement plan in 2011. The National Health Plan 2011—2020 aims to target the rural and urban poor in hopes of achieving the development goals it made with the Visions 2050 plan. The goal is to provide greater and better access to care for underserved populations. The government aims to significantly increase Papua New Guinea's rank in the UN Development Programme's Human Development Index by 2050.

Papua New Guinea has also recorded instances of the Zika virus as of 2016. Conveyed by mosquitoes and the transmission of certain bodily fluids like blood, the Zika virus affects the development of fetuses in the womb. The virus leads to damaged brain development and undeveloped heads in utero.

Malnutrition is also a factor in many deaths because people with weakened immune systems do not respond well to treatment for even simple illnesses. It is the underlying cause of death for children under the age of five, and it contributes to nearly 50 percent of hospitalizations annually. Private organizations like UNICEF are working to improve the state of nutrition in Papua New Guinea. By working with the government, they are trying to reach the populations who need care and education on nutrition the most.

SCHOOLING

The national literacy rate has improved rapidly, with 64 percent of the population over the age of fifteen being able to read. When Papua New Guinea gained its independence, the government expressed two goals concerning education: universal education at the primary level and access to higher education for as many as possible.

The first six years of education start at age seven in community-based schools. In remote areas, these schools are sometimes open-air, palm-thatched structures, and having them around does not guarantee enrollment. Most instruction takes place in English and in pidgin, although a small percentage of children in elementary schools learn to read and write in Tok Ples, the local language, in hopes of preserving the cultural heritage, until grade three, when English instruction begins. According to UNICEF, as of 2013, only one in three children complete their basic education.

The University of Papua New Guinea in Port Moresby, the University of Technology in Lae, the University of Goroka, and the University of Vudal provide higher education, along with the Christian Divine Word University and the Pacific Adventist University. Colleges of technical and vocational education, such as teaching and nursing, exist in most provinces, aligning with the governmental push toward technological development by 2017.

INTERNET LINKS

https://www.facebook.com/humansofpapuanewguinea
Humans of Papua New Guinea is a social media project on Facebook that brings the lives and people of Papua New Guinea to the world.

http://ebrary.ifpri.org/utils/getfile/collection/p15738coll2/id/130017/filename/130228.pdf
The 2015 Nutrition Country Profile provides a unique infographic that shows the effects of malnutrition on the country's population.

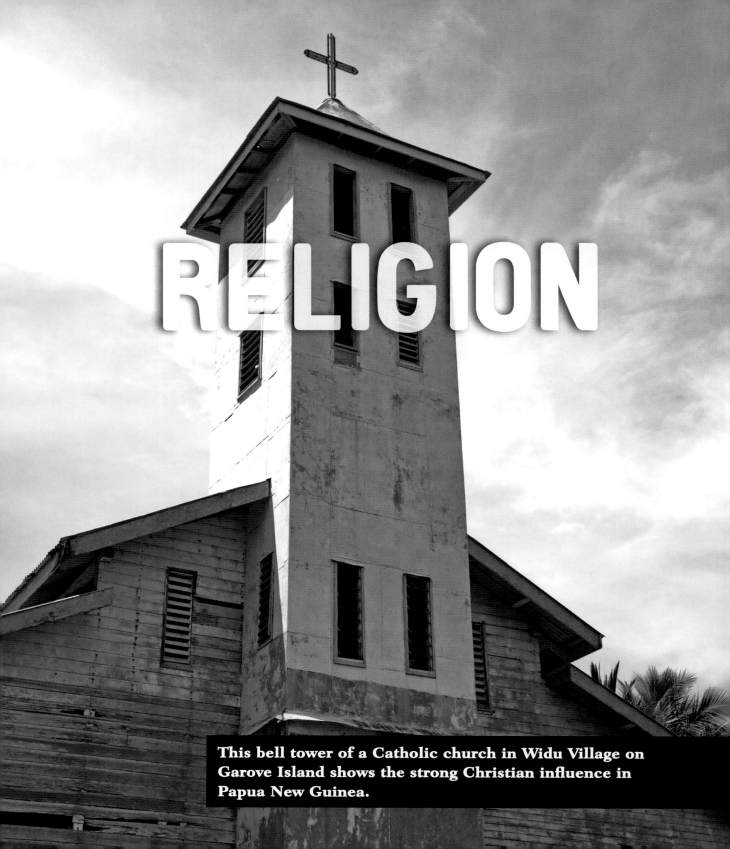

RELIGION

This bell tower of a Catholic church in Widu Village on Garove Island shows the strong Christian influence in Papua New Guinea.

PAPUA NEW GUINEA IS A LAND OF magic, spirits, and faith. However, the diversity of the different cultural and ethnic groups can be seen almost everywhere but religion. In the past, in the words of Prime Minister Michael Somare, "Papua New Guinea had not one or two, but hundreds of traditional religions, just as the nation today continues to have hundreds of tribes and hundreds of languages." Today, however, Christianity has become the main religion of the country.

The magic and spirits of traditional faiths have been looped into modern Christianity, and more than 96 percent of the population identifies as Christian. There are some people who practice traditional spirit-based faiths, some Baha'i, some Buddhists, and some Muslim practitioners, but at its heart, Papua New Guinea is a Christian nation.

CHRISTIANITY IN PAPUA NEW GUINEA

Christianity was introduced early in the country's history during contact between the local people and the outside world. Christian missions were set up throughout the country, close to and working with the local

Animism is the belief that people and other things, both living and nonliving, have spirits (like a soul) that need to be respected and, in some cases, revered. It is a component of many different religions, and most Papua New Guineans are animists. An example of animism in Papua New Guinea can be found in the ceremonial masks of tribes of the Sepik River, which are believed to be imbued with the powers of spirits. The belief in spirits is animism in action.

people. The influence of the various churches was such that by 1960 Papua New Guinea had become a predominantly Christian country.

The major Christian churches and organizations represented are Roman Catholic, Lutheran, United Church, Seventh-Day Adventist, Anglican, Baptist, and Pentecostal, along with the Evangelical Church Alliance and the Salvation Army. People who practice Christianity practice clan rituals as well as attend church without experiencing any apparent conflict of ideals. Today, however, many people who identify as Christian do not participate in church activities regularly.

GRIEF, DEATH, AND CANNIBALISM

Papua New Guinea's current laws support the right of the individual to practice his or her beliefs freely, though some limitations apply. One instance that is no longer practiced but was once part of indigenous peoples' traditions is cannibalism, or the eating of human flesh. Cannibalism was practiced for centuries by groups such as the Hewa and the Fore. It was a form of mourning or protected against witchcraft. Eating the flesh of deceased clan members who died of natural causes or disease was believed to protect against illness and to release the spirit of the deceased from the body. These groups believed that a spirit that was not released was doomed to spend its days in a sort of limbo. At one time it was considered an honor to partake in this practice.

Hostility toward the *guvmen* (GUV-men), or government, which declared this practice illegal, led to the Hewa region in the southern highlands closing to outsiders until 1965.

The ultimate end of cannibalism came with the discovery in the 1950s of kuru, or fatal laughing disease, which shuts down the central nervous system. Kuru is contracted through the consumption of certain human flesh. In tribes of Papua New Guinea, mostly women or children contracted the disease. When scientists informed them of the cause of the disease, people found it challenging to accept that a traditional practice was making them sick. However, once it was accepted, the practice began to die out. The disease, however, was slow to manifest in some cases, and so a study was put in place to monitor people with kuru. In 2009, the last person known to have kuru died, and by 2012, the kuru epidemic had ended.

SACRED SPACES

Christian churches and mission houses are present throughout Papua New Guinea and vary widely in design and complexity. Urban centers tend to have larger churches constructed in a modern Western manner, while in rural areas they can be simple halls made from whatever local materials are available.

The other important religious space is the clearing in the village, where all types of dances, singing, and communal rituals take place. The rituals enact traditional stories and beliefs, prepare people for important events, or try to bring about a desired outcome. Taboos and traditions dictate the form and proceedings of these rituals, including the costumes and the body paint used, the words sung, the music played, who participates, and even the food consumed.

ISLAM IN PAPUA NEW GUINEA

There is a small Islamic population in Papua New Guinea. The nation's first mosque was built in Port Moresby in the 1980s. In recent years, there has been an increase in conversion. Between 2001 and 2007, the number of practitioners increased form 479 to over 5,000. Though still strongly in the minority, such a rise in numbers shows the effect that intercultural contact can have on a population.

The Sepik River region is dotted with examples of traditional belief in the shape of large, cone-shaped haus tambarans *(house TAM-bor-ans), or spirit houses. These spirit houses are sacred male spaces that hold traditional ceremonial and religious artifacts and tools. The houses are forbidden to women, who are believed to have their own magic and power and therefore are not allowed to enter. In fact, it is believed that a woman, should she*

cross the threshold of one of these sacred spaces, will die. It is a male space, used to celebrate male rites of passage and decorated with elaborate masks and totems. Fertility rites, magical ceremonies, and male initiations take place here.

SUPERNATURAL BELIEFS

A feature of Melanesian society is widespread belief in magic, practiced by ordinary people for beneficial reasons (for example, to aid healing, ensure successful harvests, and gain victory in war). Sorcerers, however, wield it for power. The magic practiced by the ordinary people through their superstitions and daily rituals permeates all areas of village life. The magic of sorcerers is veiled in secrecy and fear, and disease and misfortune are attributed to the workings of enemy sorcerers. In some societies, women use the men's fear of their witchcraft to manipulate them.

SPIRITS

The most important spirits are usually those of ancestors, but in some areas, nonhuman spirits feature more prominently. These may be perceived in

For decades, sanguma, *also known as witchcraft, was a serious offense in Papua New Guinea. Today, many still believe in the power of sorcery and witchcraft, and many people suffer each year from accusations of performing sorcery or witchcraft. In 1971, the Sorcery Act was passed, which stated: "There is a widespread belief throughout the country that there is such a thing as sorcery and that sorcerers have extraordinary powers that can be used sometimes for good purposes but more often for bad ones, and because of this belief many evil things can be done and many people are frightened or do things that otherwise they might not do." Sorcery was criminalized, and the Sorcery Act was often used as a defense in murder cases.*

In modern society, vulnerable, poor women are often accused of practicing witchcraft, although not all sorcery or witchcraft is considered bad. If accused and targeted, this results in severe, violent beatings.

The rising disparity in wealth often leads people to make accusations of witchcraft. Accusing someone of witchcraft is a great way to target someone, possibly for their land or their resources. Vigilante justice encourages mobs to attack the accused, leaving their resources available for the taking. In some cases, an accusation of witchcraft could be equal to a death sentence.

The Sorcery Act was repealed in 2013, but that has not stopped villages from targeting women—in some cases, their own family members.

animal or monster forms. For example, people living near the Sepik fear the crocodile *masalai* (mass-ah-LAY), or spirit, and offerings of *buai* (bwai)—betel nut—are thrown into treacherous rapids inhabited by the *masalai*. Such spirits are believed to have individual personalities and are thought to have the ability to communicate their anger or goodwill. People take great care to please the spirits, believing that they can affect the fortune of an individual or a tribe, and this forms an integral part of ritualistic beliefs and practices.

Birds play a significant role in these traditions. For the Dani clans in the highlands, each clan has ties with a particular bird species and considers it to be a clan member. To the Enga in the western highlands, different bird species are inhabited by ghosts, and hearing their call requires certain

behaviors to avert personal disaster or to prevent the ghosts from attacking. Note that not all spirit animals are evil. Some spirits are thought to bring about bountiful crops, successful hunting, and personal achievement. However, beliefs regarding spirit animals are slowly being transformed as Christianity spreads, education reaches more people, and the skeptical ways of the modern world take on a greater influence.

ORAL TRADITIONS

Singing and dancing are not only entertainment but also important methods of handing down oral histories to succeeding generations. They provide a means of committing information to the communal memory in the absence of written records. Songs are composed for important events like initiations and funerals, and to commemorate victories. During the planting of crops or the construction of houses, for example, both the men and the women sing, by themselves or in unison. In the highlands, a single voice sometimes rings out down the green hillside, followed by the response of chanting voices of all ages from nearby areas.

Some evenings, people gather around the fireside to sing and dance. This is often accompanied by storytelling. The storyteller is greatly respected, and many tales deal with the existence of good and evil, the origin of special foods, family ties, warfare, the beginning of humankind, how people came to inhabit their region, and the origin of the tribe or the clan. Such evenings are also the time to discuss day-to-day events and exchange news. Often the dividing lines between magic, religious beliefs, clan histories, and social ceremonies are difficult to distinguish. Many of the people's festivals and arts are expressions of their religious beliefs.

The green betel nut is chewed recreationally as a mild stimulant. Betel nuts are shown here at the Page Park Market on New Britain Island, along with mustard sticks.

INTERNET LINKS

https://www.beautifulmosque.com/Port-Moresby-Mosque-in-Papua-New-Guinea
These are images of the mosque in Port Moresby.

http://www.new-guinea-tribal-art.com/wp/index.php/2014/01/26/sepik-mask
New Guinean art is tied to religion, and masks from the Sepik region are both beautiful and imbued with supernatural powers of protection.

LANGUAGE

Women from Kerema, Papua New Guinea, visit with one another while in town.

9

LANGUAGE IS THE PERFECT PLACE to see the diversity of Papua New Guinea. There are over eight hundred different languages spoken in the relatively small country. According to the translation agency Pangeanic, this diversity translates to "a language for every 8,563 Papua New Guineans." The rough terrain of Papua New Guinea kept people separate and allowed for incredible language divergence to the point where neighboring tribes may speak entirely different languages. Some languages are spoken by no more than a few hundred people, and others face possible extinction for how rarely they are spoken.

ENGLISH IN PAPUA NEW GUINEA

When the country came under Australian governance, English was used in administration and education, and it was subsequently adopted as the official language of Papua New Guinea because of its commercial utility. Today it is the language of government, education, commerce, and higher levels of administration, but it is not spoken on a national scale. It is spoken only by the percentage of the population who have access to formal education.

CREOLE LANGUAGES

Hiri Motu, a language developed by the Motu for their trading expeditions in the Gulf of Papua and thus used outside its original borders, was adapted by the Armed Native Constabulary to become Police Motu in British New Guinea. It became a lingua franca for people in the region until the introduction of English. Difficulties in communication remained, however, and in the absence of a common language that would be easy for speakers of many tongues to adopt, a pidgin, Tok Pisin, developed in the late nineteenth century to fill the gap.

Tok Pisin is a mixture of English, German, and Melanesian words set within a Malay grammar pattern that is easy to pick up. It has around 1,300 words that do the equivalent work of 6,000 words in English. It is sometimes called Neo-Melanesian or Melanesian Pidgin, Papua New Guinea Pidgin, or Tok Boi. The language arose among the Melanesian people who were hired as plantation laborers in Australia and the Pacific. Other regions of the Pacific have their own pidgins.

Some words, especially verbs, have strong German origins, but Tok Pisin is based heavily on English, and this influence is increasingly felt. For example, a towel used to be called *laplap bilong waswas* (LAP-lap BEE-long WAS-was), or "cloth for washing," but is now referred to simply as *taul* (TAH-ol). Other words

TOK PISIN

Transcription of the traditionally spoken Tok Pisin is a phonetic process based on English sounds and letters and has a minimum of pronunciation rules. The first syllable of the word is usually accented, unless the word has a suffix, in which case the suffix is stressed. Letters that are not heard are not written, so that "paper," for instance, is pepa *(PEH-pah), and "sugar" is* suga *(SOO-gah). Some letters are interchangeable, such as* f *and* p, *and* b *and* v. S *does the job for* sh, ch, *and even a soft* r. *Pronunciation and word usage can vary from region to region, but the similarities allow for comprehension.*

Some of the many varied languages spoken in Papua New Guinea are endangered and face possible extinction. The small tribal populations have trouble keeping languages alive; there are fewer people to pass on the language. As older generations die without teaching younger generations, different words and parts of the language are lost. Eventually, a language can become critically endangered or die off with the last known speaker of a language. "Critically endangered," an official designation by UNESCO, means that a language's "youngest speakers are grandparents and older, and they speak the language partially and infrequently." Examples of critically endangered languages in Papua New Guinea are Bilakura, Kamasa, Abaga, and Laua.

from geographically close languages such as Indonesian have crept in, and many modern Australian colloquialisms have been integrated into the vocabulary, making for colorful speech. *Naiswan* (NAIS-wan), for instance, comes from the Australian "nice one" and is used to express congratulations or approval.

Tok Pisin is a highly effective language that is living, growing, and evolving some of its own features. It has largely replaced Motu, the former lingua franca around the southern Papua area.

MEDIA

Radio is the principal medium for broadcasting in a country that has relatively low literacy rates and where information is traditionally passed on orally. The National Broadcasting Corporation was set up in 1973, and it operates a national shortwave station, AM and FM radio stations out of Port Moresby (largely in English), and provincial services in Tok Pisin, Motu, and other regional languages. Most of the nation receives these broadcasts, which offer regional, national, and sporting news; community announcements; religious programs; and entertainment and local music.

Papua New Guinea's first television station started in 1987, when broadcasting stations were established in Port Moresby, Lae, and other centers. Papua New Guinea has a free broadcast television station, EMTV.

People with expensive satellite dishes or cable television, however, are able to watch Australian, American, Indonesian, and Malaysian programs. Videos are also popular, and they are available from trade stores, hotels, and *kai* shops, or food stores. Despite television's popularity, television sets are still reasonably rare, and are predominantly found in Port Moresby and urban centers.

Papua New Guinea has used a postal system since 1886, when the SS *Victory* carried mail between Australia and New Guinea. Today, an extensive postal system is in operation. People collect their mail from post offices and regional post agencies set up in trade stores. Domestic mail is carried by air, sea, and road, and airmail carried within the country does not incur any extra fees. Delivery of mail, along with that of people and supplies, to remote areas is carried out by air.

The country's urban centers have a fully automated telephone system, while in the remote areas connections are powered by solar energy. The radiophone is operator-connected to the very remote areas. There are no area codes, with direct dialing between centers. Cell phone technology is taking off in Papua New Guinea, providing people with an expensive but important means of communication. As of 2016 there were about 3.3 million cell phone users.

The internet is also being adopted to access written information and to communicate by email. Governments, businesses, and organizations are increasingly launching their own websites. Internet use will continue rising thanks to social media and smartphones. Both tools are starting to equalize internet usage and grant more people access to the web and each other. There were about 900,000 internet users in 2016.

PRINT MEDIA

The country has a few popular newspapers. The oldest, the *Post-Courier*, predates the country's independence with a start date in 1969. The *National* proclaims itself the top-selling newspaper in Papua New Guinea, and the *Wantok* is a Tok Pisin paper. There is also an online newspaper know as *PNG Facts*. Unfortunately, there have been some changes to the freedom of the press in the twenty-first century, including greater censorship and the closure of the Australian Associated Press's Papua New Guinea office in 2013. The closure of the Australian Associated Press office was the result of insufficient funds, but the unfortunate loss of the international perspective is notable. Furthermore, the media took another hit in 2013 when Prime Minister Peter O'Neill served a reporter at EMTV, one of the nation's top media sources, with a defamation lawsuit over the reporter's corruption allegations. There were also rumors that the station's broadcasting license was threatened by O'Neill, though O'Neill denied that allegation.

Reading is becoming popular as more people proceed to higher levels of education and literacy rates rise. The availability of books is fair in urban centers, where bookshops, libraries, and schools are located, but accessibility is poor elsewhere. Many schools, organizations, and government offices maintain their own small library collections. There are significant research-level libraries at universities, and the National Library Service collects books, photos, and items of national and historical interest.

Print news is still popular in Papua New Guinea. Here a man relaxes against a wall while reading the *Post-Courier*.

INTERNET LINKS

http://www.languagesandnumbers.com/how-to-count-in-tok-pisin/en/tpi
Visit this website to learn to count in Tok Pisin.

http://www.thenational.com.pg
This is a link to the *National*, one of the more widely read newspapers in Papua New Guinea.

http://www.unilang.org/course.php?res=80
Readers can explore and learn the basics of Tok Pisin at this website.

ARTS

A market stand displays brightly colored masks from the Sepik River region for sale.

10

ART IN PAPUA NEW GUINEA IS a diverse blend of modern and traditional talents. Papua New Guinea's art forms are often traditional and practiced in the course of daily living, but they are also used to show the new identity of the country. As a relatively young nation, Papua New Guinea has spent the years since independence forming a cultural identity, and art plays a huge part in that. As described by the East-West Center, the contemporary art scene is a means to create a new national identity. Contemporary art combines traditional images and patterns with modern themes and mediums.

Some art forms, like body painting, are more about religion, tradition, and celebration than about the act of making art. For example, nonpermanent body paint and body adornment for festivals and celebrations are expressions of art, but they are not designed to last forever. In other instances, efforts are being made to preserve national artwork. The National Museum and Art Gallery is in charge

"Thousands of years in the making, the culture of Papua New Guinea is unique and untouched. In the remote villages visitors will find tribes that passionately maintain traditions through art, initiations and sing sings." —Papua New Guinea: A Million Different Journeys website

Papua New Guinea is rich with festivals and big events, which are often celebrated with sing-sings (SING-sings). Members of the community sing and dance for hours at such a celebration. The events can go on through the evening and for many days at a time, with participants dressed in bright colors, body paint, and traditional feathers and animal skins. The dances often retell traditional stories or address new themes. Sometimes sing-sings are very heavily influenced by ritual; other times they can be more spontaneous. Preparation for the dancers can include fasting or restricting themselves to traditional foods, staying inside the village enclosure, and speaking only with the initiated men. Though a traditional practice, sing-sings have become a way of maintaining peace between different villages and tribes, as well as huge tourist attractions.

of administering the National Cultural (Preservation) Act, designed to keep artifacts from leaving the country and to help create a national artistic identity. The Institute of Papua New Guinea Studies is also involved in preservation by researching all facets of traditional culture. Documenting traditional music, folklore, myths, and dances through writing, audio recording, photographs, and video ensures a continued tradition in the arts. New works join those from the past to create a complex heritage of art and beauty.

RITUALISTIC MUSIC

Singing, chanting, and dancing are integral parts of a villager's daily life. They remain essential elements of religious rituals and indispensable components of every festival. Drums are the main musical instruments used. Rhythmic drumming resounds at all celebrations, and the drums are artworks in themselves. The *kundu* (KUHN-doo), seen on the national coat of arms, is a small drum carved from a hollow wooden cylinder, narrow in the middle and wider at each end, resembling an hourglass. It is played with one hand. It often has a handle and may have seeds, feathers, or other kinds of ornamentation.

Wind instruments are common, varying widely by region in construction and the sounds produced. In one area of the Sepik, a series of eight long conical horns are played. In the highlands, pottery flutes such as the ocarina, a globular clay flute, are made. Sacred flutes that are made in male and female pairs and are never played separately are usually saved for initiation rites. There is also a small flute played with the nose, and other types of flutes are made in various parts of the country from reeds or bamboo.

Horns and shells are sounded around the country; in some coastal areas, they are used to send warnings or other messages up and down the coast. Bullroarers, another instrument found in some areas, are swung around on a length of cord and make a loud, eerie, moaning hum. New Britain has a musical bow made from a strip of palm with a string of vine, and people in the highlands created a small harp-like instrument. The *lanaut* (LAH-nowt) from New Ireland is played for its range of bird and other animal sounds.

A Raun Raun Theatre Group dancer takes part in the Festival of Pacific Arts while wearing traditional, brightly colored garb and accessories.

THE ARTISTIC COMMUNITY

Around the time of Papua New Guinea's independence, interest in the arts flourished. Music students at the National Arts School, founded in 1972, studied both Western and Melanesian instruments, and many chose to synthesize the two. In 1990, the school merged with the University of Papua New Guinea. From the National Arts School, successful groups emerged. The rock band Sanguma was the first to succeed with its Tok Pisin and Tok Ples songs and its homegrown blend of traditional and contemporary Western instruments and rhythms. It was very popular both at home and internationally, paving the way for other popular Papua New Guinean artists such as George Telek, Patti Potts Doi, Painim Wok, Barike, and Paramana Strangers. In Port Moresby, private clubs play modern jazz or blues music, and there are discotheques in the larger towns.

Performing traditional songs and dances comes naturally to Papua New Guineans and is a big part of tourism. Performances of traditional songs and dances were some of the topics of Papua New Guinea's early theater. Even today, highland shows and festivals draw many different tourists to see

Mathias Kauage, born in Papua New Guinea in 1944, would grow up to become one of the forerunners of modern art in the Pacific region. A self-taught artist, Kauage grounded his work in island culture and Papua New Guinea's history. His early work revolved around Chimbu myths, while his later work explored daily life in Port Moresby, Papua New Guinea's independence, and the country's history. Many of his works are beautiful paintings characterized by bold, bright uses of color, but his copper reliefs are just as incredible. Made by impressing images on sheets of copper, these reliefs are works to behold. The later works are signed "Kauage—Artist of PNG" [Papua New Guinea]. Kauage passed away in 2003, but his legacy as "The Artist of Papua New Guinea" is still seen in contemporary art.

the beauty of traditional celebration. As for theater, Seeds Theatre Group, formed in 1997, is a theater troupe that uses art as a means of social learning. Their productions are geared toward solving social issues by spreading knowledge to potentially illiterate communities through theater. Examples of this include AIDS/HIV and other STI education, as well as the pandemic violence against women.

The Raun Raun Theatre, based in Goroka, has similar goals. In many ways, the Raun Raun captures the essence of modern theater's importance, with the goal to "help overcome social problems that did not exist in traditional society." Theater is effective in this because the people of Papua New Guinea relate to storytelling; it has always been a feature of their lives.

VISUAL ART

Apart from spectacular and colorful body embellishment, some groups of Papua New Guineans practice the visual arts via carving and painting. The Hewa people from Southern Highlands Province make ocher paintings on flat sheets of bark. These are created to gain power over the ideas or animals represented on them, particularly before hunting. They are not displayed as decoration but instead are stored in small thatched shelters until they deteriorate.

This act protected the cultural property of Papua New Guinea to aid in artifact preservation and cultural heritage preservation. In order to create a cultural identity, the people of Papua New Guinea needed to both create and protect a cultural heritage in tangible artifacts. The law covers the following content:

(a) any object, natural or artificial, used for, or made or adapted for use for, any purpose connected with the traditional cultural life of any of the peoples of the country, past or present; and

(b) any mineral specimen or fossil or mammal remains of scientific or historic interest to the country; and

(c) any other collection, object or thing, or any collection, object or thing of a class, declared to be national cultural property … and

(d) any collection of national cultural property

People in other regions traditionally carved storyboards from fragile bark. Today they construct these in a sturdier manner, depicting various village events in relief. In Gulf Province, *gope* (GOH-peh) and *hohao* (HOH-how) boards are beautiful shield-shaped carvings traditionally kept in the men's houses. They were thought to contain the spirits of ancestors or heroes and guardians of the village. Today, they are more commercial and are made for tourists in only a few communities. They are carved with stone axes from the old wood of canoes. Cassowary bones and shark teeth are used to create finer details, and they are colored with paints made from burnt shells (white), charcoal (black), and clays (reds and browns).

The Sepik River is often called the River of Art. Along the river, many things used by the people daily are lavishly decorated. Canoes, for example, are carved with decorative prows representing animals or people. Spirit

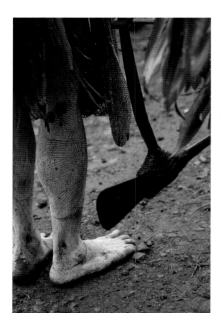

A performer in the Mount Hagen sing-sing carries a ceremonial ax.

masks, shields, and other large carvings are everywhere, and even clay bowls and cooking pots are decorated. On the Trobriand Islands, carving produces ornate and useful walking sticks, stools, and small tables, sometimes inlaid with mother-of-pearl. Shell jewelry, particularly if made from valuable black coral, is popular in the coastal towns. The art of carving is displayed in finely crafted bowls made from dark wood polished with a pig's tusk. The rims of some are patterned with the coastal themes of fish and turtles.

WAR AND ART

The creation of decorative weapons, shields, and masks throughout Papua New Guinea demonstrates the link between art and daily living. Weapons and shields have long been decorated for ceremonial occasions, and they help create the fearsome look of a warrior in full regalia. Stone axes in the Mount Hagen region are worn across the back and only have ceremonial value. Their slate blades are attached to the wooden handles with decorative woven-cane strips. Some stone axes are etched with geometric motifs.

Sharp bone daggers, including those made of the valued cassowary bone, are worn as ornamentation. The Huli make small picks tipped with the slicing claws of cassowaries. Spears are bedecked with a variety of fiber bindings, feathers, and shells, as well as with incised designs. Shields are endowed with a spiritual symbolism that is just as important as the physical task of defense. They are highly valued by Western art collectors, as special care is taken in carving and decorating them.

The masks of Papua New Guinea show great diversity in styles and materials, ranging from wood to turtle shell, and their size can span from 12 inches (30 cm) in length to 47 inches (119 cm). Masks from some areas look almost African, but the Sepik spirit masks are as distinctive as the rest of the carvings from that region. They are carved from wood, then covered in molded clay that has been embedded with teeth (mostly from pigs), hair, and shells. Some masks are used exclusively by male secret societies and may be woven from pith.

MODERN RADIO

Papua New Guineans enjoy a variety of music, including the contemporary hits that play on the radio in the United States, as well as island reggae. Dance and music are a regular part of life, and artists like rapper O-Shen and reggae singer Anslom Nakikus have found success among the many popular artists playing on the radio in Papua New Guinea.

WOVEN ART

Bilums are the colorful woven net bags seen nearly everywhere in Papua New Guinea. They are traditionally made from natural materials such as rattan, dried leaves, grasses, and strong pandanus fiber. Modern materials such as plastic and nylon are also used, with an even more colorful result. The bags are strong, versatile, and carry anything from a baby to loads of firewood. The process of making them is time consuming, and most of the weaving is done by women.

INTERNET LINKS

https://www.artstret.com/Papua-New-Guinea-Artists
This gallery showcases and sells art from some of the leading contemporary artists working in Papua New Guinea.

http://museumpng.gov.pg/index.php/www/home
Explore traditional art and artifacts of Papua New Guinea through the National Museum and Art Gallery.

http://streema.com/radios/country/Papua_New_Guinea
Listen live to Papua New Guinea radio through streema.com.

LEISURE

Evenings bring time for rest and conversation, as these people depicted here are doing in Port Moresby's Capital Quarter.

11

PAPUA NEW GUINEA IS A LAND OF hard work. Between farming for sustenance and having a limited income for necessary goods like food and clothing, people do not dedicate much time to fun and relaxation. Women work days gathering food, water, and firewood. In fact, according to the World Bank, "women do 70 percent of the work in agriculture." For recreation and a little extra money they make handicrafts like *bilums*. Recreation in villages is sitting around the fire and listening to stories or singing in the evenings. Men do have a bit more free time between hunting and work to enjoy each others' company, chew betel nuts, and smoke, but they, too, work hard. In the cities, the hours are long and work fills a lot of the time as well.

Urban areas offer a range of activities beyond restaurants and private clubs, which are frequented only by expatriates and those with money. Port Moresby is described by Lonely Planet as "expensive, dangerous … not easily walkable," but also as a city that "may well grow on you." This is a common description of most urban areas. The large, young population of the urban poor experiences the city quite differently from the wealthy. For them, small social gatherings among family and friends, with a meal included, are sometimes held—an urban version of the rural custom of gathering around the fire. Radio and television provide both entertainment and information for those with access to them, and movies are screened publicly in some towns, but there is not much money for a lot of leisure activities.

Market days in the towns and the villages are opportunities to trade, shop, and talk with friends. Hotels and discotheques provide evening entertainment in the larger towns, although their numbers are limited. In towns, there are clubs for all sorts of outdoor activities, including team sports, bush walking, sport fishing, boating, and diving.

BANNING BETEL NUTS

Betel nut, or *buai*, is the green nutlike fruit of the areca palm, which is chewed for its mildly stimulant effect. This effect is increased with the addition of lime powder that acts as a catalyst. The chemical reaction between the *buai* and the lime produces a bright-red liquid accompanied by copious saliva.

Indiscriminate spitting means that the red liquid often ends up on pavements around town. The long-term chewing of betel nut causes the mouth to be dyed a bright red, while the teeth are permanently blackened. The practice can lead to mouth cancer. In 2009, the government began restricting betel nut chewing by banning the practice. Chewing betel nut, however, is a part of the culture, and police have trouble stopping people from trading and chewing the nuts.

SPORTS

The concept of team sports came to Papua New Guinea with Europeans. Prior to their arrival, competitions in traditional skills—such as canoe races and displays of prowess in hunting, fishing, or other skills—were conducted by many groups, often with a sing-sing or feast. Christian missionaries introduced many team sports that required minimal equipment, and these rapidly gained popularity. As a result, most of the sports played in Papua New Guinea have a foreign origin, although boating, swimming, and skin diving are not far removed from traditional activities.

As this woman's mouth shows, chewing betel nut stains the teeth and gums bright red.

"Football" refers to three separate games, of which rugby is the most popular. The play is rough, but no one seems to mind. Large games can turn into a sort of tribal warfare on the field and sometimes give vent to underlying feelings of hostility. The spectators, who are passionate about supporting their favorite team, may join in, and violence can erupt. Rugby is played at the international, national, and local levels. Australian rules football, known as Aussie rules, also has its adherents in the country, as does soccer, which is sometimes called football as well.

Dancers in a sing-sing dress up as mudmen of the Asaro Valley and dance while covered in clay. They represent the dead men from legend.

Basketball, netball, softball, volleyball, and baseball are popular throughout the country, and are sports in which women are more likely to participate. Other Western sports such as tennis, cricket, bicycle racing, and rock climbing are also enjoyed.

MYTH IN THE HIGHLANDS

Sing-sings are also a part of recreation. One famous legend enacted in Asaro sing-sings revolves around the mudmen. It is said that warriors of the Mut tribe were driven back by their enemies into the nearby river. They emerged

HIGHLAND SHOWS

In the early days of the highland shows, which started in the 1950s, as many as forty thousand warriors in full regalia would congregate and dance with their paints, feathers, and weapons flashing in the sun. Traditional dancing and singing accompany brightly painted bodies and traditional grass skirts and headdresses. The shows are an annual occurrence and act as tourist events. The show performers are patient and very willing to be photographed. One of the most famous and largest of the shows is the Goroka show. The Goroka show began in 1957 and takes place in mid-September. It acts as a way to celebrate Independence Day. More then 140,000 people attend the show to see the dancing and listen to the songs and kundu *drums.*

later, ghostly pale due to their covering of dried mud. Their enemies mistook them for evil spirits and fled in terror. This legend is relived by the dancers, who cover their bodies in gray mud that, as it dries and flakes, represents the decaying flesh of the dead. Large rounded mud masks complete the illusion.

There are high rates of malaria in lowland areas of Papua New Guinea. Infection can lead to greater risks while playing sports. For example, malaria leads to enlarged spleens that can rupture during high contact, making the game more dangerous. Love of the game, however, far outweighs risk, and football and high-contact sports continue to be played.

INTERNET LINKS

http://www.asaromudmen.com/gallery.html
This website contains many pictures of and additional information about the Asaro people and their mudmen.

http://www.pngrfl.org
The Papua New Guinea Rugby Football League's official web page has many statistics and current information about the team and its members.

FESTIVALS

Performers dance and sing while dressed in full ceremonial regalia at the Garoka sing-sing.

12

PAPUA NEW GUINEA IS FAMOUS for its festivals. Festival guests and tourists will encounter lively music in the form of beating drums, masked warriors, and slow, fluid dances, among many other things. Holidays like Independence Day are celebrated with festivals and sing-sings. Each region has its own celebrations for different things, such as the Yam Harvest Festival in the Trobriand Islands during the summer months, and the Warwagira and National Mask festivals in Rabaul each July. Often festivals are to celebrate spiritual and traditional beliefs, but they can also be about gift giving and exchange with neighbors or other groups.

INDEPENDENCE DAY CELEBRATIONS

Papua New Guineans celebrate Independence Day on September 16. While various ceremonies and shows are held all over the country, the

"Today, the sing-sings provide opportunities for PNG's assorted tribes to show off their traditional dress (bilas), stage warrior dances, share ancient stories of the spirit world, and perform their ancestral songs ... These amazing gatherings are folk festivals at their very best, and there's no more valuable way to immerse yourself in the local culture." —Meg Boyd, *GOWay* travel blogger

Kula exchanges include the giving of shell necklaces as a sign of goodwill and friendship between tribes.

biggest and most famous is the Hiri Moale, commemorating the ancient trading voyages made between villages in the Port Moresby area and Gulf Province.

Long before the arrival of Europeans, *hiri* were conducted amid ritual procedures. The Motu people in the Port Moresby area made clay cooking pots that they traded for sago in the Gulf Province villages, where sago was abundant. The voyages were necessary for the Motu because the dry climate of the Port Moresby area did not favor farming.

The building of the *hiri* canoes, called *lakatoi* (LAH-kah-toy-e), was supervised by two men who were honored with the role. During the building of the canoes, they had to observe strict taboos involving eating special foods, not communicating with their wives, and not washing or cutting their hair.

The canoes for the voyages were large and sturdy because they traversed hundreds of miles with able-bodied men in them. Early in its construction, the shell of each boat was blessed by a shaman using specially concocted incense smoke. Village women plaited palm fronds for the sails, and these were sewn together by the men. The sailors would leave in September. The villagers would wait fifty days for their safe return and then celebrate that return with a large feast. The festival honors their journeys still today.

KULA EXCHANGE

Another series of trading ceremonies involves a circle of islands, including the Trobriands, in and around Milne Bay Province. The early sea voyages by canoes are reenacted, although the distances covered today are not as lengthy as before. Modern vessels are sometimes used, but elaborately decorated canoes are still favored.

The exchange of goods serves the purpose of spreading goodwill among the islanders. The items exchanged are decoratively carved armbands and special necklaces called *bagi* (BAH-ghee), made with red shells that are painstakingly ground by women into evenly proportioned circular disks. The exchanges are purely ritualistic, and the goods rarely leave the trading ring. What is significant is that travelers are offered hospitality by their exchange partners. Besides the exchange of the ritual jewelry, it is also an important opportunity to trade in goods such as baskets, food, and pottery.

MOKA AND GIFT GIVING

In some areas of Papua New Guinea, preparations for huge exchanges require several years between ceremonies. One reason is to collect the appropriate number of pigs. These ceremonies are sometimes held to exchange "payback goods," but more often they are designed to display the wealth of a "big man" or a clan.

One ceremony is held to repay debts incurred and add items to the repayment. In most parts of the highlands, the ceremonies are called Moka, while the Enga, from Enga Province in the highlands, have a similar custom called the Tee. These ceremonies are accompanied by all the trimmings of a sing-sing. Goods exchanged include pigs, kina shells, and cartons of beer. Many pigs are slaughtered, and the feasting can continue for several days. The repetition of these exchanges means that at some point in time, the giver will receive similar things to what he has given and possibly more. Sometimes these events accompany marriages or other ceremonies.

CELEBRATING CROCODILES

The Crocodile Festival of the East Sepik Province is a three-day event in the first week of August that shows how important crocodiles are to the local people. Dancing and singing are used to celebrate the event, with performers dressed in grass skirts and elaborate traditional headdresses. For these people, the crocodile is a symbol of strength, power, and manhood. Men will even cut scars into their skin to resemble the crocodile as a rite of passage.

A pig feast is always a ceremonial affair, prepared according to custom. The pigs are killed with a bow and arrow, and their carcasses are placed over an open flame, after which they are removed and cut up. Clotted blood is sometimes collected in a gourd to be used later for magical purposes.

KENU AND KUNDU FESTIVAL

In Milne Bay Province, the Kenu (canoe) and Kundu Festival, begun in 2003, features the war canoes that the area is known for. Artisans carve traditional canoes using the same colors and patterns of their ancestors. It is traditionally believed that such canoes must be carved in specific ways from certain woods to please the gods. In many ways, the festival seems like a celebration of history and culture. *Kundu* drums pound out over the water as dozens of canoes row by. Up to forty warriors race one another across the bay. Awards are given to the teams that win the races. The festival also has music, dancing, and singing as a part of the festivities and celebration.

TRELLIS YAM FARMING

Yam harvests are also occasions for celebration in Papua New Guinea. As an important part of the local diet, the harvest is observed with celebration by the Abelam in the Maprik region near the Sepik. Yams are grown on distinctive trellises. The islanders pride themselves on the size and quality of the yams grown. The yams are a status symbol and speak of the cultivator's farming

YAM MASKS

The Abelam people of the Sepik region use elaborate woven masks to honor the yam harvest. These masks are not worn by the people who make them, however. The elaborate masks are placed over super-sized yams that they grow. The yams' growers will also decorate the yams with painted faces to make them look like human figures. The decorations complement the masks placed on the yams. These masks are believed to give the yams spiritual power and knowledge of the ancestors.

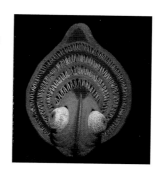

skills. Sometimes the cultivation and harvest are the sole responsibility of the men, carried out in secrecy from the women. The yams are stored in special huts, but for the harvest festival the largest yams are collected amid much ritual and singing. In a good year, some of the yams will reach a spectacular 10 feet (3 m) in length, although usually the largest ones are about 6 or 7 feet (1.8—2.1 m) long. The displayed yams are presented to the women as gifts.

INTERNET LINKS

http://indigoarts.com/galleries/yam-masks-new-guinea
The Indigo Arts Gallery shows and sells different styles of yam masks.

https://www.youtube.com/watch?v=TKpaCeA26lc
This video shows the Ambunti Crocodile Festival dance, which is elaborate and unique to the region.

FOOD

Bananas, banana leaves, and tubers are all placed in a large, natural earth oven in preparation for roasting a pig.

13

THE FOOD OF PAPUA NEW GUINEA is based on what is available. Food is farmed, and the diets of people do not vary much because of that. Most meals revolve around crops such as taro, *kaukau*, yams, sago, and pigs. Ginger is used in some parts of the country, and salt is often used for flavor and preserving meat. Proteins are important, though not always readily available. Chicken, fish, and hunted game are often parts of meals. Occasionally, crocodile flesh is eaten when available. Canned fish and rice are staples, but pigs are symbols of status and are often saved for special occasions. The fertile soil ensures that fruits and vegetables grow well and are regularly consumed.

Urban kitchens look similar to those in Western homes, but people in rural areas usually cook over open fires. Sometimes there is a special open-sided *haus-wind* (HOWS-wind) hut, where the cooking fire is located. Unglazed clay pots are used for cooking over flames, while large

Men gather large banana tree leaves to place over the hot coals and line the oven floors to create an earthen oven called a *mumu*.

feasts are prepared in a ground oven called a *mumu* (MOO-moo). Metal pans are increasingly common where once only clay pots were available.

PROTEIN AND HUNTING

Hunting is an activity enjoyed by the men. It provides a valuable addition of nutrients to the diet, particularly in areas where the staple is sago, a crop that is not high in vitamins. Shotguns and rifles are common throughout the country. Small prey like wild pigs, wild dogs, bandicoots, tree possums, wallabies, and birds are preferred targets because they are challenging to hunt.

Hunting crocodiles is challenging because they are powerful and dangerous. At night, flashlights are used to reflect the crocodile's eyes, thus dazzling it and allowing a hunting canoe to get close enough to kill it with a long harpoon, aided by a blow from an ax on a softer part of the armored creature's body. Sometimes guns are used. Daytime hunting involves skilled

hunters who use their feet to find the scaly hide of the smaller New Guinea crocodile in the clay. One hunter will duck underwater and pull the surprised and thrashing creature, while the other uses a large, well-aimed knife to kill it. Crocodile skin is quite valuable, and the meat from a large crocodile can be enough to feed a whole village.

Two men, Jonathan Kosmapa and Thomson Goyap, of Mino Village use canoes and the cover of darkness to hunt crocodiles in East Sepik Province.

Fish are smoked and cooked over an open fire in Alotau, Papua New Guinea.

Fishing is carried out more traditionally. A variety of fish and shellfish are caught and eaten, including crayfish, prawns, and crabs. Spears along with bows and arrows are popular, while some fishers use nylon nets or fishing lines. In some areas, huge basket-like traps, which are often larger than the fishermen, are woven. Smaller traps made of thorny materials are woven into a cone shape and baited. Rotenone, a poison that paralyzes the respiratory system, also catches fish when poured into the water. Fishermen simply wait for the dead fish to rise to the surface.

In New Ireland, some men attract sharks to their canoes with either their voices or a rattle made from coconut shells. A noose attached to a piece of wood is then slipped around the shark's body. Dragging this device slows the shark and tires it. Once the animal is exhausted, it is speared or bludgeoned, but it often still puts up a fight while being hauled into the canoe.

Fish and other meats are eaten freshly cooked when possible, and any surplus is salted, dried, or smoked over a slow fire.

SAGO

Sago, or *saksak* (SACK-sack) in Tok Pisin, is the starchy food eaten by all the groups of people who live in the swampy areas. It is bland, nearly pure starch, and while it provides energy, it lacks vitamins and minerals that other foods provide. Sago is important because it grows in areas where it is nearly impossible to cultivate other crops thanks to flooding and waterlogged soils.

Harvesting sago is time consuming. The sago palm grows for fifteen years, storing starch inside its trunk before it flowers. It must be harvested at that point or the starch will be converted into a massive spike of flowers, after

Papua New Guineans eat small breakfasts. Usually, this meal will include pastries, cakes, fruit, or fish and rice. Lunch, however, is the largest meal of the day and is often a family meal made from local produce and chicken or fish. Dinners are small and usually consist of leftovers from lunch.

which the palm will die. The tree is cut down by men and dragged or floated closer to the village or to a convenient clearing, where the bark is stripped. The pith inside is chopped and pulped by men. The women beat and wash the pith repeatedly with water to extract the starch; the water is collected, and the starch forms a thick, gluey mass at the bottom. It can be dried to form a flour that preserves well.

A woman from the Sepik River region pounds out sago pith in preparation for cooking.

Men in Papua New Guinea are known to buy or brew beer, but in 2010, the practice of selling and drinking alcohol was banned in the Southern Highlands. Police believed that the heavy consumption of alcohol was feeding violence between clans. In the following months and years, the ban spread further to other regions of Papua New Guinea in an attempt to quell rising violence. When the ban was put in place in Lae, rioting broke out, resulting in six people dead. Smugglers also became more active and challenging to catch in the highlands.

Mumu cooking is a slow process that usually accompanies a celebration of some sort. Everyday cooking is much faster and done over a campfire. The *mumu* method is often used to cook pork and acts much like an underground, earthen barbeque. Food can be roasted or boiled in clay pots. Proteins can be dried and smoked over a fire.

There are four ways to prepare sago. The flour can be boiled in water—or the sago can be cooked immediately before it has dried into flour—to form a thick, glutinous porridge with fish, coconut, or vegetables added. The second method is to mix the flour with a little water to form a thick pancake that is fried on both sides in a very hot pan without fat or oil. The third is to simply pour the sago into a hot pan. The sago hardens immediately and is flattened and turned over to cook on the other side. The resultant flat cakes are known as *parem* (PAH-rem) and tend to be crispy on the outside and soft and chewy on the inside. People can carry these cakes on their daily tasks and eat them when needed. Finally, people make sago dumplings to be eaten with vegetable soups.

TUBER FARMING AND SWEET POTATOES

There are many varieties of sweet potatoes, also called *kaukau*, differing in color, texture, size, and flavor. These are the staple carbohydrate source in many areas, particularly in the highlands. Sweet potatoes are quite nutritious but do not form a balanced diet in themselves. They can be roasted whole, cut up and boiled with meat and other vegetables, steamed with other food in banana leaves, or baked in a *mumu*.

Men may help prepare the garden and even help plant the *kaukau* and yams, but it is the women who tend gardens. Men prepare the fields for planting by cutting tree roots left in the field and digging the soil to loosen it.

The women break up large pieces of earth and prepare mounds of the earth for planting. They then push pieces of *kaukau* or yam vine into the mounds, leaving a small part exposed. The women attend to the weeding. When they are ready, people tend to harvest only a few sweet potatoes at a time because the damp climate causes food in storage to rot. The importance of *kaukau* in the diet is reflected in the arrangement of the garden—other crops are never accorded more than a quarter of the cultivated land.

Some sweet potato growers in the highlands found a way to grow their crops despite cooler temperatures. They build large, low mounds of soil over old vegetation, and these form the planting beds for the sweet potatoes. As the old vegetation decomposes, the compost adds vital nutrients to the soil and raises the temperature of the mounds, thus protecting the plants on cold nights.

Women, like this woman shown here planting sweet potatoes, are often in charge of preparing and planting the gardens.

In a typical Papua New Guinean garden, you might find any of the following: three or four varieties of sweet potatoes, yams, taros, starchy bananas for cooking, peanuts, long green beans, local leafy green vegetables, corn, chilies, cassavas (whose roots yield the starchy tapioca), sugarcane, ginger, pumpkins, *pitpit* cane (the flower is edible), pandani, breadfruits, papayas, and even tobacco. There are often coconut palms nearby as well.

Many of these vegetables and fruits are cooked like the sweet potatoes, but the coconut is widely included in other mixes of food. Fresh green coconut is moist and creamy in flavor. It is commonly grated into a fine mash and added directly to the pot, or the grated coconut is wrapped in a piece of coarse cloth that is squeezed tightly to extract the milk. When coconut milk is added to a meal, especially to cooked rice, the food is rich in flavor.

BANANAS

Approximately 1.3 million tons (1.2 million metric tons) of bananas are grown on about 192,750 acres (78,000 ha) annually here, and more than two hundred varieties are cultivated, some of which come in surprising colors, like orange. They can be used as both fruits and vegetables, but there is a difference between the two. The sweet, ripe eating bananas, known as *swit banana* (SWIT bah-nah-nah) in Tok Pisin, have bigger ridges on the fruit. The green, starchy cooking bananas, known as *karapua* (kah-RAH-PU-ah), are longer and paler.

Rich in carbohydrates, cooking bananas are treated like a starchy vegetable and cannot be eaten raw. They can be roasted whole in their skin, baked with coconut milk, boiled and mashed, chopped and added to stews, or sliced thinly and fried in hot oil as chips. Sweet bananas are also cooked in dishes where a sweeter flavor is wanted, such as in curries, meat dishes, or desserts, but are often eaten raw.

Other parts of the banana plant are useful as well. Banana leaves are heated by moving them around in a flame or a hot stove until they are soft and pliable, and then they are used to wrap food prior to cooking. They impart a delicate flavor as well as preserve the tasty juices of the food that is being cooked. The male bud of the banana plant can be peeled and the inner part either sliced thinly and eaten raw or boiled as a vegetable.

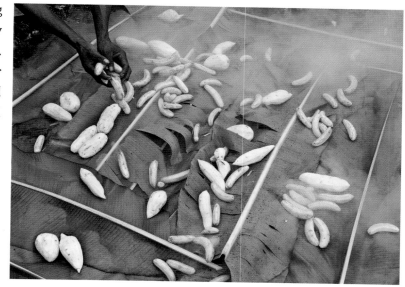

Bananas and tubers are traditional daily foods. Here they are laid out in a ground oven in preparation for roasting a pig.

INTERNET LINKS

http://www.alws.org.au/media/wysiwyg/discover-more/schools/curriculum-resources/recipes/Papua_New_Guinean_Recipesx.pdf
Interesting Papua New Guinean recipes can be found here, like yam patties and coconut with mixed vegetables.

https://www.worldtravelguide.net/guides/oceania/papua-new-guinea/food-and-drink
This travel guide describes some foods found in Papua New Guinea.

COCONUT KAUKAU

2 sweet potatoes, washed and dried
¼ cup butter, cut into pieces
½ cup coconut cream
½ onion, finely chopped
2 cloves garlic, crushed
1-inch piece of fresh ginger, grated
2 tablespoons orange juice
4 heaping tablespoons of grated cheese
Salt
Pepper

DIRECTIONS

1. Wrap each sweet potato in aluminum foil and place on a plate. Bake in preheated 400°F (200°C) oven for 1 hour, turning sweet potatoes halfway through cooking.
2. Check for doneness by poking a wooden skewer. The center should be perfectly tender. Cooking time depends on the size of the sweet potatoes. Do not hesitate to continue cooking for a few minutes if necessary.
3. When out of the oven, split sweet potatoes in two lengthwise. Gently scoop out with a spoon, place the flesh in a bowl, and immediately add the butter. Add salt and pepper, and mix well while crushing with a fork to get a smooth purée.
4. Set the skins of the hollowed half sweet potatoes on a baking sheet lined with parchment paper.
5. Add the coconut cream, onions, garlic, ginger and orange juice to the mashed sweet potatoes. Mix well.
6. Fill the hollowed half sweet potatoes with this preparation. Spread 1 tablespoon of grated cheese over each, then place them under the broiler for a few minutes, until the cheese is completely melted.
7. Serve right out of the oven, as an accompaniment to fish for example, or as a main dish with rice and a green salad. Serves four people.

BANANA CAKE

½ cup margarine or butter
½ cup of sugar
2 eggs
1 teaspoon vanilla essence
3 medium-size bananas (mashed)
1 teaspoon baking soda
1½ cups of self-raising flour
⅓ cup of milk (enough to give it the right texture—wet, but not runny)

DIRECTIONS

1. Preheat the oven to 350°F (180°C). Beat together the butter, sugar, and vanilla until creamy. Add the eggs and mashed bananas in gradually.
2. Add the baking soda to the flour. Gradually add the flour to the wet ingredients, adding a bit of milk each time. You may not need all of the milk depending on the wetness of the bananas, so do not add it all at once. The batter should be wet but not runny.
3. Pour the batter into a greased, round, 8-inch baking dish, and bake cake for 45 to 50 minutes.

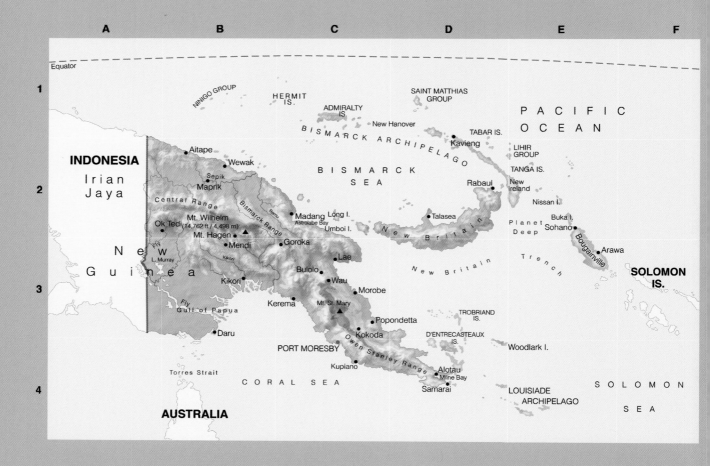

A   B   C   D   E   F

Equator

1

NINIGO GROUP

HERMIT IS.

ADMIRALTY IS.

SAINT MATTHIAS GROUP

New Hanover

TABAR IS.

PACIFIC OCEAN

BISMARCK ARCHIPELAGO

Kavieng

INDONESIA

Irian Jaya

Aitape

Wewak

Sepik

Maprik

Central Range

Bismarck Range

BISMARCK SEA

LIHIR GROUP

TANGA IS.

New Ireland

Rabaul

Nissan I.

2

Mt. Wilhelm

Ok Tedi (14,762 ft / 4,498 m)

Mt. Hagen

Mendi

Kikori

Madang

Astrolabe Bay

Long I.

Umboi I.

Ramu

Goroka

New Britain

Talasea

Planet Deep

Buka I.

Sohano

New

Guinea

Fly

L. Murray

Bulolo

Lae

Wau

Morobe

New Britain

Trench

Bougainville

Arawa

SOLOMON IS.

3

Kikori

Kerema

Mt. St. Mary

Popondetta

TROBRIAND IS.

Fly

Gulf of Papua

Daru

Kokoda

D'ENTRECASTEAUX IS.

Woodlark I.

PORT MORESBY

Owen Stanley Range

Kupiano

Alotau

Milne Bay

Samarai

LOUISIADE ARCHIPELAGO

SOLOMON SEA

Torres Strait

CORAL SEA

4

AUSTRALIA

MAP OF PAPUA NEW GUINEA

Admiralty Islands, C1
Aitape, B2
Alotau, D4
Arawa, E3
Astrolabe Bay, C2
Australia, B4

Bismarck Archipelago,
   C1—C2, D1—D2
Bismarck Range, B2, C2
Bougainville, E2—E3
Buka Island, E2
Bulolo, C3

Central Range, A2, B2
Coral Sea, B4, C4

Daru, B3
D'Entrecasteaux Islands,
   D3—D4

Equator, A1, B1, C1, D1, E1,
   F1

Fly River, A2, B2—B3

Goroka, C3
Gulf of Papua, B3

Hermit Islands, B1, C1

Indonesia, A1—A3
Irian Jaya, A1—A3

Kavieng, D1—D2
Kerema, C3
Kikori, B3
Kikori River, B3
Kokoda, C3
Kupiano, C4

Lae, C3
Lake Murray, A3, B3
Lihir Group, E2

Long Island, C2
Louisiade Archipelago, D4,
   E4

Madang, C2
Maprik, B2
Mendi, B3
Milne Bay, D4
Morobe, C3
Mount Hagen, B2
Mount Saint Mary, C3
Mount Wilhelm, B2

New Britain, C2, D2-D3
New Britain Trench, C3, D3,
   E3
New Guinea, A1—A3,
   B2—B4
New Hanover, C1
New Ireland, D2, E2
Ninigo Group, B1
Nissan Island, E2

Ok Tedi, A2, B2
Owen Stanley Range,
   C3—C4, D4

Pacific Ocean, E1—E2,
   F1—F3
Planet Deep, E2—E3
Popondetta, C3
Port Moresby, C4
Rabaul, D2
Ramu River, B2,
   C2—C3

Saint Matthias Group, D1
Samarai, D4
Sepik River, B2
Sohano, E2
Solomon Islands, F3—F4
Solomon Sea, E4, F4

Tabar Islands, D1—D2
Talasea, D2
Tanga Islands, E2
Torres Strait, B4
Trobriand Islands, D3

Umboi Island, C2

Wau, C3
Wewak, B2
Woodlark Island, D4,
   E4

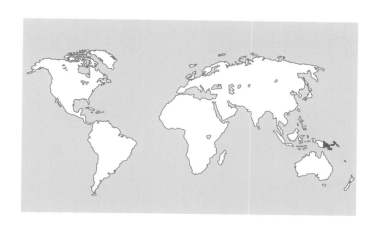

ECONOMIC PAPUA NEW GUINEA

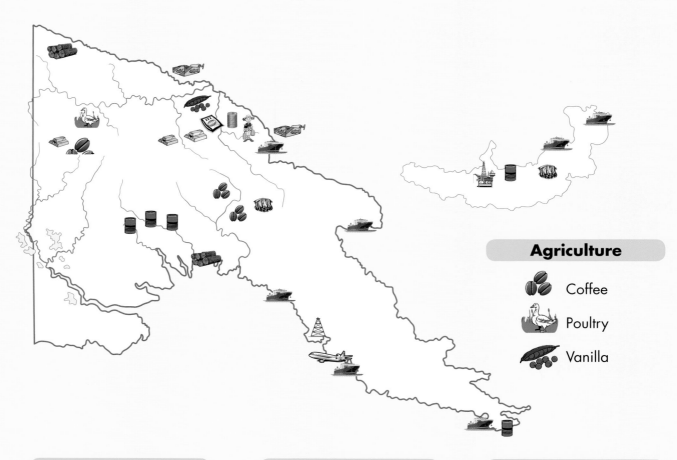

Agriculture

 Coffee

 Poultry

 Vanilla

Manufacturing

 Petroleum refinery

 Cannery

 Oil refinery

 Sugar refinery

Services

 Airport

 Port

 Hydroelectricity

 Tourism

Natural Resources

 Gold

 Copper

 Silver

 Tuna

 Oil

 Lumber

ABOUT THE ECONOMY

OVERVIEW

Papua New Guinea's economy relies on income from mineral, oil, and natural gas exports, and is vulnerable to fluctuations in global commodity prices. Fishing, forestry, and agriculture are also important revenue sources, and a large portion of the population are non-waged subsistence farmers. Concerns over tribal violence, crime, and corruption have limited the private sector, and the country continues to require foreign aid.

GROSS DOMESTIC PRODUCT (GDP)
$19.92 billion (2016 estimate)

GROSS NATIONAL INCOME PER CAPITA
$3,500

EXTERNAL DEBT
$22.04 billion

FOREIGN AID RECEIVED
$546.3 million

FOREIGN RESERVES
$1.629 billion

INFLATION (CONSUMER PRICES)
6.3 percent

CURRENCY
1 kina (K) = 100 toea (t)
K 3.16 = US $1 (2016)

PERCENTAGE OF EXPORT INCOME (2012)
41 percent fuels and mining products, 23.8 percent agricultural, 6.2 percent manufactures, 29 percent other

MAJOR EXPORTS
Minerals, timber, coffee, palm oil, cocoa, copra, crayfish, prawns, gold, copper ore

AGRICULTURAL PRODUCTS
Coffee, palm oil, cocoa, copra products, tea, rubber

MAJOR IMPORTS
Machinery and transportation equipment, manufactured goods, food, fuel, chemicals

MAIN EXPORT PARTNERS
Australia (15.9 percent), Japan (17.4 percent), China (12.1 percent)

INDUSTRY
Copra processing; palm-oil processing; plywood production; wood-chip production; chicken and fish canneries; mining of gold, silver, and copper; crude-oil production; petroleum refining; construction; tourism; ecotourism

WORKFORCE
4.365 million

UNEMPLOYMENT RATE
Total unemployment: 2.5 percent
Urban unemployment: as high as 80 percent

POPULATION BELOW POVERTY LINE
37 percent

CULTURAL PAPUA NEW GUINEA

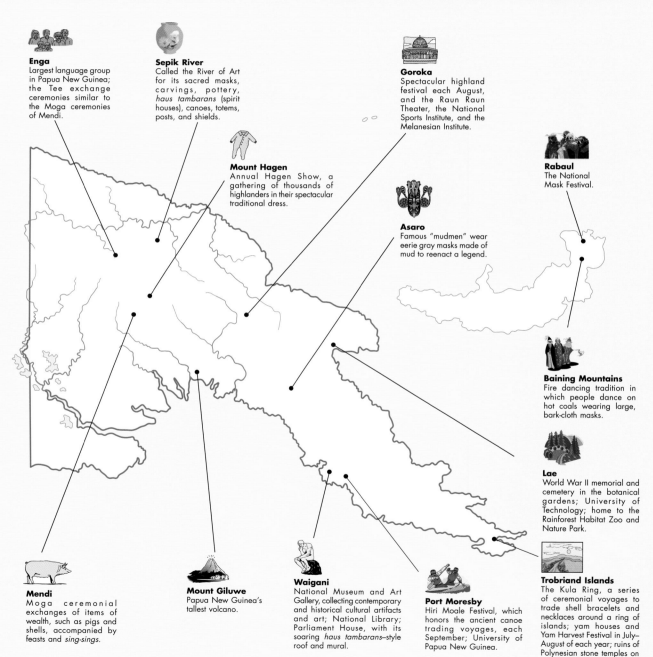

Enga
Largest language group in Papua New Guinea; the Tee exchange ceremonies similar to the Moga ceremonies of Mendi.

Sepik River
Called the River of Art for its sacred masks, carvings, pottery, *haus tambarans* (spirit houses), canoes, totems, posts, and shields.

Goroka
Spectacular highland festival each August, and the Raun Raun Theater, the National Sports Institute, and the Melanesian Institute.

Mount Hagen
Annual Hagen Show, a gathering of thousands of highlanders in their spectacular traditional dress.

Asaro
Famous "mudmen" wear eerie gray masks made of mud to reenact a legend.

Rabaul
The National Mask Festival.

Baining Mountains
Fire dancing tradition in which people dance on hot coals wearing large, bark-cloth masks.

Lae
World War II memorial and cemetery in the botanical gardens; University of Technology; home to the Rainforest Habitat Zoo and Nature Park.

Mendi
Moga ceremonial exchanges of items of wealth, such as pigs and shells, accompanied by feasts and *sing-sings*.

Mount Giluwe
Papua New Guinea's tallest volcano.

Waigani
National Museum and Art Gallery, collecting contemporary and historical cultural artifacts and art; National Library; Parliament House, with its soaring *haus tambarans*–style roof and mural.

Port Moresby
Hiri Moale Festival, which honors the ancient canoe trading voyages, each September; University of Papua New Guinea.

Trobriand Islands
The Kula Ring, a series of ceremonial voyages to trade shell bracelets and necklaces around a ring of islands; yam houses and Yam Harvest Festival in July–August of each year; ruins of Polynesian stone temples on many islands.

ABOUT THE CULTURE

OFFICIAL NAME
Independent State of Papua New Guinea

LOCAL NAME
Papuaniugini

NATIONAL SYMBOL
Bird of paradise perched on a *kundu* ceremonial drum, with a barbed spear behind the drum

NATIONAL FLAG
It is diagonally divided from the top of the hoist to the bottom of the fly; the yellow bird of paradise is centred on the upper red triangle; the white Southern Cross constellation is centred on the lower black triangle.

NATIONAL ANTHEM
"O Arise, All You Sons"

LAND AREA
174,850 square miles (452,860 sq km)

POPULATION
Around 8 million

CAPITAL
Port Moresby

REGIONAL CENTERS
Lae, Madang, Wewak, Goroka

NATIONAL/OFFICIAL LANGUAGES
English is the official language; Tok Pisin and Motu are widely spoken.

TOTAL LANGUAGES
839 distinct language groups

ETHNIC GROUPS
Papuan, Melanesian, Negrito, Micronesian, Polynesian

LITERACY RATE
64.3 percent

LIFE EXPECTANCY
65 years for men
69.5 years for women

MAJOR RELIGION
Christianity

IMPORTANT HOLIDAYS
New Year's Day (January 1), Good Friday and Easter (March/April), Queen's Birthday (mid-June), Remembrance Day (July 23), Independence Day (September 16), Christmas Day (December 25), Boxing Day (December 26)

TIMELINE

IN PAPUA NEW GUINEA	IN THE WORLD
50,000 years ago The first people are believed to arrive on the New Guinea mainland.	
17,000–10,000 years ago A gradual rise in sea levels covers the original land links with Australia.	**600 CE** Height of Mayan civilization.
	1000 The Chinese perfect gunpowder and begin to use in warfare.
1526 CE Portuguese captain Jorge de Meneses sights the coast and names it Ilhas dos Papuas.	
1546 The Spaniard Iñigo Ortiz de Retes lands on the northeastern part of the mainland and names the land Nueva Guinea.	**1558–1603** Reign of Elizabeth I of England.
1793 Britain claims the island of New Guinea.	**1776** US Declaration of Independence is signed.
1828 The Dutch claim the western half of New Guinea.	**1861–1865** The US Civil War.
1873 Port Moresby is named.	
1906 The British protectorate is handed over to the independent Commonwealth of Australia and renamed Territory of Papua.	
1914 Germany loses its colony when the area is occupied by Australian forces.	**1914–1918** World War I.
1921 The former German colony is renamed the Territory of New Guinea.	**1939–1945** World War II.
1942 Japanese occupation begins in both Australian New Guinea territories.	
1949 Australia joins its two territories under the name Territory of Papua and New Guinea.	

IN PAPUA NEW GUINEA	IN THE WORLD
1963 Indonesia is granted control of West New Guinea.	
1964 The First House of Assembly is formed.	
	1966 The Chinese Cultural Revolution.
1968 The Second House of Assembly is formed.	
1973 On December 1, the territory obtains self-government.	
1975 On September 16, the new constitution takes effect. Papua New Guinea is independent.	
1977 The first full election since independence is held.	
1989 Civil war begins in Bourgainville.	
	1991 Breakup of the Soviet Union.
1995 The Bougainville Transitional Government is put in place. Prime Minister Theodore Miriong is sworn in.	
1996 Bougainville prime minister Theodore Miriong is assassinated and replaced by Gerard Sinato.	
	1997 Hong Kong is returned to China.
1998 An Australian-led peace monitoring group helps oversee a permanent cease-fire in Bougainville.	
2001 The Bougainville Peace Agreement is signed.	**2001** Terrorists crash planes in New York, Washington, DC, and Pennsylvania.
	2003 War in Iraq begins. SARS breaks out in Hong Kong.
2011 Prime Minister Michael Somare retires. Parliament elects Peter O'Neill as acting prime minister.	
2014 A warrant for the arrest of Prime Minister Peter O'Neill is issued. He fights the accusation in multiple court cases and is not arrested.	**2016** The Zika virus breaks out and spreads around the globe. United Kingdom approves Brexit from the European Union. Donald Trump is elected president of the United States.
2017 Civil unrest breaks out in response to the 2017 elections when Prime Minister Peter O'Neill wins.	

GLOSSARY

bilum (BILL-uhm)
A strong, woven string bag made and carried by women.

buai (BWAI)
A betel nut.

guvmen (GUV-men)
The government.

haus tambarans (house TAM-bor-ans)
A "spirit house" storing items of cultural and religious significance.

hiri (hih-REE)
An ancient trading expedition.

kaukau (KOW-kow)
A sweet potato.

kenu (KEH-new)
A canoe.

kundu (KUHN-doo)
A drum featured on Papua New Guinea's coat of arms.

laplap (LAP-lap)
A loincloth or piece of cloth.

masalai (mass-ah-LAY)
A spirit.

Moka (mocha)
A large celebration where gifts are exchanged between big men.

montane
A biogeographic region just below the timberline in an upland area.

Motu
A language originally used by the Motu people in the Port Moresby region, now more widely spoken.

mumu (MOO-moo)
An oven dug into the ground.

naiswan (NAIS-wan)
An expression of congratulations or approval, derived from the Australian phrase "nice one."

omak (OH-mak)
Kina shells worn on a length of string threaded between two holes in the shell and used in trade and barter.

parem (PAH-rem)
A sago pancake.

sing-sing (SING-sing)
Any large celebration with feasting, music, and dancing.

taul (TAH-ol)
A towel.

Tok Ples
The native or local language.

Visions 2050
A national plan for growth and development in the coming decades.

wantok (WAN-tohk)
A system of reciprocity that emphasizes sharing and mutual help among families, clans, or tribes; derived from the English phrase "one talk."

FOR FURTHER INFORMATION

BOOKS

Carlson, Melody. *Notes from a Spinning Planet—Papua New Guinea*. Colorado: WaterBrook Press, 2007.

Connell, John. *Papua New Guinea*. London, UK: Taylor & Francis, 2007.

Corazza, Iago, and Greta Ropa. *The Last Men: Journey Among the Tribes of New Guinea*. Vercelli, Italy: White Star, 2008.

Montgomery, Sy. *Quest for the Tree Kangaroo: An Expedition to the Cloud Forest of New Guinea*. Boston, MA: Houghton Mifflin, 2006.

Owen, Stanley. *Papua New Guinea History and Culture: Travel and Tourism*. Roubaix, France: La Provence, 2017.

Rannells, Jackson, and Matatier, Elesallah. *PNG Fact Book: A One-Volume Encyclopedia of Papua New Guinea*. South Melbourne, Australia: Oxford University Press, 2005.

WEBSITES

BBC News: Country Profile—Papua New Guinea, http://news.bbc.co.uk/1/hi/world/asia-pacific/country_profiles/1246074.stm.

Embassy of Papua New Guinea to the Americas, http://www.pngembassy.org.

Muturzikin.com, http://www.muturzikin.com/cartesoceanie/oceanie2.htm.

The National, http://www.thenational.com.pg.

Papua New Guinea: A Million Different Journeys, http://papuanewguinea.travel/usa.

Papua New Guinea Parliament, http://www.parliament.gov.pg

Papua New Guinea *Post-Courier*, http://www.postcourier.com.pg.

Tok Pisin Translation, Resources, and Discussion, http://www.tok-pisin.com.

World Population Review, http://worldpopulationreview.com/countries/papua-new-guinea-population.

MUSIC

Nakikus, Anslom. *Pee N Gee*. 2014.

O-Shen. *Saltwater Messenger*. 2011.

Telek, George. *Amette*. 2004.

FILMS

Mueller, Dominique. *Papua New Guinea*. Filming Biosphere. amazon.com, 2017.

Nairn, Charlie. *Ongka's Big Moka: The Kawelka of Papua New Guinea*. Disappearing World. youtube.com, 1974.

Owen, Chris. *Bridewealth for a Goddess*. Institute of Papua New Guinea Studies: Ronin Films, 1999.

Warth, David. *Papua New Guinea*. Travel Wild. amazon.com, 2012.

BIBLIOGRAPHY

Alfred, Charlotte. "The Shocking Reality of the Sexual Violence Epidemic in Papua New Guinea." *World Post*, March 5, 2017. http://www.huffingtonpost.com/entry/papua-new-guinea-sexual-violence_us_56d9fca1e4b0ffe6f8e974f2.

"Biodiversity in Papua New Guinea." Coolearth.org, October 2, 2015. https://www.coolearth.org/2015/10/biodiversity-in-papua-new-guinea.

Boyd, Meg. "Discover Tribal Culture in Papua New Guinea." *Globe Trotting*, February 13, 2016. http://blog.goway.com/globetrotting/2016/02/discover-tribal-culture-in-papua-new-guinea.

Corazza, Iago, and Greta Ropa. *The Last Men: Journey Among the Tribes of New Guinea*. Vercelli, Italy: White Star, 2010.

"The Country with the Highest Level of Language Diversity: Papua New Guinea." Pangeanic, 2016. https://www.pangeanic.com/knowledge_center/country-with-the-highest-level-of-language-diversity-papua-new-guinea.

Galing, Karl. "Papua New Guinea: Improving Water and Sanitation in the Land of the Unexpected." The World Bank, November 18, 2016. http://blogs.worldbank.org/eastasiapacific/papua-new-guinea-improving-water-and-sanitation-land-unexpected.

Garret, Jemima. "Losing Papua New Guinea's Rainforest." ABC News, March 9, 2016. http://www.abc.net.au/news/2016-03-08/papua-new-guinea-rainforest-clearing/7231148.

"Introducing Port Moresby." Lonely Planet. http://www.lonelyplanet.com/papua-new-guinea/port-moresby/introduction.

"Manufactoring." IPA Papua New Guinea. http://www.ipa.gov.pg/agriculture/manufacturing.

"New Guinea People." WWF Global, 2017. http://wwf.panda.org/what_we_do/where_we_work/new_guinea_forests/area_forests_new_guinea/people_new_guinea_forests.

"Ok Tedi, Papua New Guinea." WWF Global. http://wwf.panda.org/what_we_do/where_we_work/new_guinea_forests/problems_forests_new_guinea/ mining_new_guinea/ok_tedi_forest_new_guinea.

"Papua New Guinea." *2017 Index of Economic Freedom*. The Heritage Foundation. http://www.heritage.org/index/country/papuanewguinea.

"Papua New Guinea & Wantok System." *IPI Indo Pacific Images*. http://www.indopacificimages.com/index.php/papua-new-guinea-2/papua-new-guinea-the-wantok-system.

Papua New Guinea Department of Minerals. http://www.mineral.gov.pg.

"Papua New Guinea Food and Drink." World Travel Guide, 2017. https://www.worldtravelguide.net/guides/oceania/papua-new-guinea/food-and-drink.

"Volcanoes of Papua New Guinea (67 Volcanoes)." Volcano Discovery. Accessed June 5, 2017. https://www.volcanodiscovery.com/papua-new-guinea.html.

INDEX

INDEX